THE TRUST TRIANGLE

HOW TO MANAGE HUMANS AT WORK

MATTHEW DAVIES

BALBOA.PRESS

A DIVISION OF HAY HOUSE

Balboa Press books may be ordered through booksellers or by contacting:

Balboa Press
A Division of Hay House
1663 Liberty Drive
Bloomington, IN 47403
www.balboapress.co.uk
1 (877) 407-4847

Because of the dynamic nature of the Internet, any web addresses or links contained in this book may have changed since publication and may no longer be valid. The views expressed in this work are solely those of the author and do not necessarily reflect the views of the publisher, and the publisher hereby disclaims any responsibility for them.

The author of this book does not dispense medical advice or prescribe the use of any technique as a form of treatment for physical, emotional, or medical problems without the advice of a physician, either directly or indirectly. The intent of the author is only to offer information of a general nature to help you in your quest for emotional and spiritual well-being. In the event you use any of the information in this book for yourself, which is your constitutional right, the author and the publisher assume no responsibility for your actions.

Print information available on the last page.

ISBN: 978-1-9822-8147-2 (sc)
ISBN: 978-1-9822-8149-6 (hc)
ISBN: 978-1-9822-8148-9 (e)

Library of Congress Control Number: 2020905618

Balboa Press rev. date: 04/22/2020

CONTENTS

PREFACE

The Problem

Trust is the foundation of all meaningful relationships, yet 70 per cent of professionals don't trust their managers (Engage for Success, 2013). Seventy per cent! It's a number that actually surprises few but profoundly concerns most of the awesome thought leaders alive today. From Simon Sinek to Patrick Lencioni, Paul Zak to Brené Brown, all agree that a lack of trust is the root of faltering relationships and mediocrity at work.

What galvanised me to write this book was the lack of tools to address this appalling problem. There wasn't a clear—or, more importantly—practical roadmap for building trust that centred on one of the most important relationships at work—you and your manager. I work with managers every day, and it was this dilemma that necessitated the development of this program. By implementing *The Trust Triangle*, you can now offer teams an environment where you (the manager) and they (your team) can genuinely flourish at work, unburdened by the baggage of a *people manager* without *people management* skills. At the moment you're probably (inadvertently) weighing your team members down and holding them back. The great news is you can change that. However, change has an ambitious agenda with an onerous adversary.

A formidable problem that devours any kernel of trust is apathy. It stealthily dominates the workplace and shows itself in disconnection, indifference, disregard, and detachment of self and others. Apathy (in this context) is often your IQ (intellectual quotient) response to EQ (emotional quotient), and apathy particularly thrives on ignorance of the importance of (or an arrogant attitude towards) emotional intelligence. This becomes apparent when a successful team member is promoted to team leader. It's often those with low EQ who refer to it as 'the fluffy stuff' or 'soft' skills. If no appropriate training/coaching is given on managing humans at work, apathy naturally kicks in, and another team leader stacks up the 70 per cent pile of ill-equipped managers, cocking up countless team members' work lives.

> Indifference is the strongest force in the universe. It makes everything it touches meaningless. Love and hate don't stand a chance against it.
>
> **—Joan D. Vinge**

Successfully managing people is a skill and something I passionately believe can be learned. I have demonstrated this with hundreds of team leaders. Very few instinctively have the skills that are necessary, but most can and do learn these skills if properly nurtured in a program like *The Trust Triangle*. Don't be fooled by any nonsense that suggests giving effective feedback, setting clear expectations, and acquiring the many other skills *The Trust Triangle* brings to life are skills we innately possess. These critical skills can be acquired. Of course, they are developed through experience, but without a solid foundation, unskilled managers are damaging innumerable amount of relationships and therefore seriously curtailing business growth.

And here's the business case in a nutshell. According to a massive study by Gallup, managers account for at least 70 per cent of the variance in employee engagement scores (Beck & Harter, 2014). That dovetails perfectly with another large study by Engage for Success. They're the folks who found that 70 per cent of professionals don't trust their managers (Engage for Success, 2013).

They also discovered that companies with low engagement scores earn an operating income 32.7 per cent lower than companies with more engaged employees (MacLeod & Clarke, 2009). And what did Engage for Success recommend as an enabler for success? Yep, engaging managers.

Wow! Manager behaviour really does affect the bottom line—not by a percentage point here or there but by over 30 per cent! I was baffled as to why this wasn't addressed until I looked more deeply. There are two reasons. First, apathy stops leaders from fundamentally dealing with trust. They like the word on their websites but not in their hearts, and most importantly, it's just not consistently demonstrated in the workplace.

> We want the facade of a relationship without the work of a relationship.
>
> **—Ujwal Singh**

Second, when leaders do want to make a change, too many management programs skim through trust and are more interested in an operational perspective of management. Your IQ loves logic. Human emotions and behaviour are often baffling to the IQ and therefore disregarded and ignored. No amount of rationale can fully explain the emotions of human beings, so our IQ dismisses them at work and hopes emotions will simply be turned off by professionals and therefore any emotional disturbance will simply go away. But it doesn't, and that apathy continually threatens the foundations of trust.

Many thought that apathy at work had been abandoned to the history books—when a stiff upper lip didn't mean too much Botox but rather an emotionally suppressed fellow who was applauded for disregarding his feelings. However, beware: the latest generations are finding connection with others to be a real challenge. In every office, I see grads preferring to walk around the office with their heads down and headphones in (especially in tech). Apathy masked as focus or apathy masked as introversion—the list is long. My apathy-detection monitors have been finely tuned over the years, and I guarantee you that when apathy is high, collaboration is low.

The Solution

> No one can whistle a symphony.
>
> —Halford E. Luccock

Managers are the conduits between the leaders of an organisation and their workforce. I have focused on managers for this reason as they are the delegators, deliverers, operators, administrators, educators, mentors, and evaluators (among other duties). This program, however, is equally powerful for team members to grasp. I've taught *The Trust Triangle* to customer service reps, data scientists and salespeople, so please don't hold back from sharing *The Trust Triangle* with team members across your business to help them understand the powerful ingredients that build trust at work. There is absolutely no reason to use this methodology in stealth mode, so please, share it far and wide in your organisation.

Unlike with other management/team leader training programs—the goals of which are wide, varied, and often unfit for the modern workplace—the focus of this book is laser sharp. I will demonstrate how to *build trust at work to increase performance*. By using clearly defined steps that are simple to implement and powerful when practised, you can become an outstanding people manager.

I will introduce you to three key domains of trust transformation: empathy, energy, and expertise. Empathy is often the least practised but can have the greatest impact. Beware, though—it is often misrepresented. Empathy is not about being 'nice'. It's neither weak nor soft. True empathy is a frickin' superpower! It's a real driver for trust and gives team leaders the ability to have meaningful conversations which are usually avoided at work. Empathy also contextualises communication and encourages a growth mindset as well as prioritising the development of people and processes. Apathetic people managers (from CEOs down) can see team members as a 'number' in a 'role' instead of human beings with all the needs of a human being. As already mentioned, many employers ignore learning and mastery, preferring professionals to somehow struggle through—a clear example of apathy and a fixed mindset. I remember sharing an article on LinkedIn from HBR entitled 'We Wait Too Long to Train Our Leaders' (Zenger, 2012). This was a conversation I had with one connection:

> Manager: I was a regional manager at 26 before I had any training for the role. Made it work!!
>
> Matthew: Interesting. You said you 'made it work'—could you tell me more? How did you know what to do? Just guess? Were you mentored?
>
> Manager: I learned on the job. There was some mentoring, but the company didn't really believe in L&D. I made many mistakes, but over two years I had it refined by self-teaching.
>
> Matthew: Thank you for your honesty.

Unfortunately, this is not an unfamiliar story in the workplace. When I read 'made it work', it really intrigued me, just as much as the double exclamation marks, so, as you can see, I dug deeper. I don't know who I felt sorry for the most. I felt despondent for the people he had to manage while he made 'many mistakes', and I was saddened but not surprised that he had been left high and dry by his leaders because they didn't 'believe' in L&D. Sure, we learn on the job and will all make mistakes, but let's try to lessen those blunders instead of showing indifference to poorly equipped managers! Tragically, this story is very common.

Apathy is a neglecter and an evader; it frequently fails to deal thoroughly with emotional issues. The net result is a low commitment to the business and, therefore, an inefficient workforce that will cost the company millions. According to the 2019 State of Workplace

Empathy Study by Businessolver, 93 per cent of employees say they're likely to stay with an empathic employer (Businessolver, n.d.). In the same study, 92 per cent of CEOs said their organisation was empathic, but only 72 per cent of employees agreed! Although the idea of empathy is embraced by leaders, empathy in action is a very different story. These figures show a clear disconnect. That, my friends, is apathy! Otherwise, they'd have done something about it! Empathy in action is apathy's kryptonite.

This book is a holistic response to the fact that most awesome professionals promoted into management roles are left stranded by leaders who are not investing in the skills to manage humans. To those leaders who are investing, I salute you. You are the leaders I learn from as you demonstrate a growth mindset as well as the empathy to understand that new responsibilities often require new skills, especially when dealing with humans!

No matter how good you are as a developer, marketer, or accountant, it doesn't set you up for managing human beings. You're about to embark on an adventure that is going to positively change your life at work. Before you start this intrepid journey, I want to spell out the benefits of working *The Trust Triangle* into your work life. It's well worth keeping these front of mind. They'll keep you motivated.

First of all, at the end of each chapter, there are clear instructions, called 'Tools'. Don't expect any categorical change without any categorical action. There's also a checklist for change at the end of the book which lists all the top tips, tools, and techniques that have been mentioned throughout the book. Be consistent with this action, and I promise that you will see tons of benefits manifesting.

They include the following:

- An understanding of the basics. You'll understand the role, relationships, and responsibilities of a manager.
- Insight and tools to understand what really motivates people at work. From creating the right culture to celebrating

success, you'll have techniques to blow apathy out of the water, and you'll have the tools to replace apathy with a vibrant and productive workplace.

- A significant increase in emotional intelligence. You'll manage your emotions much better due to a tangible improvement in your self-awareness and the tools to manage relationships with others.
- A massive increase in your communication skills. You'll gain the ability to handle conflict through effective feedback skills and the ability to influence and make an impact. You'll learn how to manage meetings as well as manage up.
- Brilliant delegation skills with the know-how to increase accountability (in yourself and others) and encourage autonomy.
- Better recognition of others to increase performance.
- Tools to coach and mentor your team members.

So, rev up your inner engine and let's do this!

Note: any references in this book pertaining to 'team leader' or 'manager' are interchangeable and mean the same thing. The term 'manager' can feel like an echo from a bygone era, hence our more preferred wording 'team leader'. Also, I consult for businesses that primarily work in an office environment. Therefore, this book has been written specifically with that setting in mind.

Trust is the glue of life. It's the most essential ingredient in effective communication. It's the foundational principle that holds relationships.

—Stephen Covey

ACKNOWLEDGEMENTS

I see myself as a practitioner, and I want to personally thank all the thought leaders and visionaries mentioned in this book. I have created a practical methodology based on their research and insights. Without their wisdom this book would not have been possible.

I want to also thank every manager I have coached, trained, and worked with. All your feedback has honed this book, and I thank you for your enthusiasm and encouragement.

Some people I'd particularly like to call out include Tracy Paterson and Viv Bowra, who really helped me in so many ways. Thanks to Kate Delamere, who is an excellent writer, and my editors, Christina McIntyre and Caroline Clough, for their invaluable feedback. Massive thanks to Balboa Press for all their support, and special thanks to my designer, Grant Ware, and my assistant, Mateja Kovac, two of the most patient men I have ever met. Finally, massive thanks to Paul Jones, an epic Chief People Officer who has been a friend and mentor and Nigel McNeil, who has been super supportive throughout this project.

TRUST

Introduction

Seventy per cent of professionals don't trust their manager (Engage for Success, 2013). What a woeful piece of feedback from team members about their supposed advocate, confidant, and mentor. Ever wondered why productivity is low and stress so high? Look no further. Only a pitiful 30 per cent of us trust in one of the most important relationships of our daily lives. Imagine if only 30 per cent of the computers in your office worked properly, if the others' software hadn't been updated for a decade, keys stuck, and screens flickered. There'd be an uproar! Yet, when it comes to managers, companies (especially start-ups and SMEs) do little or nothing to help reverse this terrible statistic.

> **Definition: trust**—a firm belief in someone or something. *Synonyms:* confidence, belief, hope, faith, assurance, reliance.

Look at all those priceless characteristics from confidence to hope. Please do not underestimate the dominion of trust. It is the foundation of all meaningful relationships. That doesn't change because you're in a workplace. Trust is the cornerstone of successful collaboration, whether you're a developer depending on the word of a designer, a dancer about to launch off a pedestal backwards, or a driller depending on a colleague's land survey to avoid cutting through a live 20,000-volt electricity cable.

> A team is not a group of people who work together. A team is a group of people who trust each other.
>
> **—Simon Sinek**

Simon Sinek is a visionary and thought leader who I admire greatly. In his talks, he rightly states that leadership is a choice and not a rank. He says that you can be given authority over others who will do as you say because you have that 'authority', but that doesn't mean they will follow you. And it's said that leaders without followers are just going for a walk! To follow is to believe in that leader and therefore trust them. You don't earnestly follow those you don't trust. Those you do trust, you back. They are the ones you deeply connect to and enthusiastically wish to collaborate with.

In his fantastic book *The Five Dysfunctions of a Team*, Patrick Lencioni identifies 'absence of trust' as the basal problem for failing teams (Lencioni, 2002). In an annual survey from PWC, most CEOs noted that a lack of trust constituted *a foundational threat* to their companies (Craig, 2017). Trust is central to your success as a team leader.

Trusting people on their word used to actually mean something in societies. Now it's more often scoffed at and seen as being a little naive. Back in the day, the difference was that someone's word was their bond and not some dodgy display of manipulative insincerity; a marvellous grouping of words by the ever-brilliant Kim Scott from her book *Radical Candor* (Scott, 2018) which burns through trust like fire through kindling as self-interest trumps helping others.

It's time to give trust its honour back and show how sacred and invaluable it really is. The most powerful way to improve trust is to get to know and connect with your team members. Connection drives trust. Disconnection drives distrust. This is elementary but consistently ignored at work. The idea that we have to keep a 'professional distance' by disconnecting is claptrap. There's evidence everywhere about the power of connection. People who feel more connected to others have lower rates of anxiety and depression. Studies show those who connect with others are more trusting and cooperative, and as a result, others are more open to

> Instead of putting others in their place, put yourself in their place.
>
> **—Amish proverb**

trusting and cooperating with them (Seppälä, 2012). Consumers are four times more likely to shop at a retailer when they feel an emotional connection. I could go on.

The Connection Conundrum

I'll dive into this topic later on, but get connection wrong, and you'll end up with distant and distrusting relationships at work. The best way to approach connection is to think about friendship. Connection is key to building relationships. It's how we start to build trust. We use small talk to establish whether a stranger has the same values, similar interests, and a similar background. Once connection is formed, only then can genuine trust be established. Once trust is formed, deep collaboration is achieved. Let me give you an example. You meet a stranger in your local coffee shop. You both have dogs and begin small talk around dog breeds and local walks. You share stories about your experiences with your dog. You laugh about the trials and tribulations. This is surface small talk. You part ways and over time begin bumping into one another more regularly at the cafe. You open up more about work, family, and friends. Before long, you both go on walks together, and find you have much in common. The small talk is getting profound now and connection gets stronger as your authentic self emerges. You go on holiday, and they look after your dog. You come home, and the dog is happy and well. Now deep trust is formed, and real collaboration begins. You get the keys to each other's homes and house-sit when your friends are away.

So, the normal pathway in relationships are:

1. Connection
2. Trust
3. Collaboration

But that is flipped in the workplace.

1. Collaboration
2. Trust
3. Connection

In bigger companies, you have to collaborate with strangers all the time. Even in smaller businesses, collaboration is pushed to the front before connection. Many tech start-ups have engineering teams who have little to do with other areas of the business, and collaboration with them can be difficult. Why? *Because no one has truly connected.* What happens? Collaboration is clunky because trust is shallow as connection is superficial. Just as in the dog-walker example, you're giving people the keys to your house and your much-loved dog before establishing the usual relationship requirement of connection prior to collaboration. No wonder people are suspicious and silly feuds whirl around work.

> Most people do not listen with the intent to understand. Most people listen with the intent to reply.
>
> **—Stephen Covey**

So top tip number one. Make time to connect with your team members in any way you can. Tell them about the connection conundrum and make time to purposely hang out with team members. Get to know them on a human level. Try not to talk about work and make a real effort to consistently connect.

When I ask a training group to put their hands up if they love small talk, hardly anyone raises a hand. Mistake, big mistake. This indicates a lack of understanding. Small talk is the beginnings of connection. However, merely languishing in chat about the weather is as dull as the English weather itself, so try to move through the weather chat and find things that you both have in common.

Family is one. It's important that you discover the things that are important to the other person, remember those facts, like kids' and pets' names, then move on through to deeper connection. The deeper the connection, the stronger the trust and the more meaningful the collaboration. It all starts with small talk so give your head a shake and lean into the uncomfortable. For those still worried about what to talk about, think about stuff you've watched on the telly or at the cinema. Upcoming events, such as holidays, are good subjects to chew on as you lay the foundations for a meaningful relationship. Do not miss this step. When I dig into a problem at a client's business, the root cause of poor collaboration is often a lack of connection. That, in turn, makes trust feeble, unsteady, and susceptible to breaking down.

I remember spending tons of time and money developing a 'Trust Insights Report'. I hoped this would definitively show managers the stark truth around the lack of trust at work. However, when testing this report, every single manager came out with amazing results. They were trust powerhouses! I was baffled. I tried it in another company, and the results were again inordinately high. Knowing the research and seeing the opposite results opened my eyes to what is really going on in the workplace. The team members scoring their managers were doing so based on the thin veneer of trust built on their time, purely collaborating. They were not considering real trust. They were frankly ignoring the power of true connection that they experience with their loved ones and good friends. Although my insights report is now redundant, the process revealed a revelation that empowered this book. We're starved of deep trust at work by just playing in the paddling pool of collaborative trust because we're not diving deeper into connection. When we take the leap and really connect, deep trust emerges, and awesome collaboration begins. If you've ever experienced shallow trust at work, compared with deep trust, you'll need no convincing.

We *can* connect at work. Sure, it's a different scenario to home life, but we humans are complex beings who deal with all kinds of different relationships. We're more like kaleidoscopes than kettlebells! The way we relate to our mums and dads is very different from the way we relate to our husbands or wives. The way we deal with children is different from the way we deal with adults. We are amazingly flexible creatures, so don't think you have to turn off your humanity at work. It's not a binary choice. A professional relationship is just another shade of the many relationships we already have. Becoming curious about family, passions, or pets helps us to connect and therefore care more. When we care more, we go the extra mile. When we care less, we become careless. It's simple.

Lots of companies purport to be the leading lights of trust. I see 'trust' emblazoned on their business websites as a core value, but they merely scratch the surface, and many talk the talk and are not prepared to take the action required to build genuine trust. They are hoodwinking top talent into the shallow waters of artificial harmony. Please, if you don't give a damn about employee engagement, at least have the decency to steer away from fake facades and empty promises.

Apathy

I see experienced managers who couldn't care less, and it leads to poor results. It's no doubt been your experience that if you don't trust someone, you'll keep your distance, remain cautious, and certainly not go the extra mile. Why do we think that's an awesome modus operandi at work? If not addressed, distrust destroys empathy, sucks the energy out of productivity, and erodes any chance of innovation.

So, why the heck are we not taking urgent action to fix this? Well, it's sad but simple: we're hardwired to apathy.

Apathy. Best defined as disinterested, dismissive, and detached. My goodness, those words can define many a manager I've met in the past. People try to be 'professional' by detaching from their empathy and disregarding human emotion, but by doing so, they become indifferent to their people and therefore their business practice. Apathy is also defined as 'the absence or suppression of passion, emotion or excitement. A lack of interest or concern for things that others find moving or exciting.' To be clear, it is indifference to the fact that we are dealing with humans. This apathy ignores the fact that humans are emotional. There is nothing impressive about being cold, emotionless, or distant at work unless you're a soldier about to kill the enemy. Most of us are not at war, yet our hardwired preference to a negativity bias means that those not practising emotional intelligence will actually use the professional environment as some deformed theatre of war and treat others in that context. Is it any wonder that teams are unnecessarily stressed out by 'combat-ready' managers with no real war to fight? Therefore, I am impressed by professionals who are self-aware, can manage their emotions, empathise, build deep relationships and not exercise an innate apathy that feeds fear, resulting in human disconnection.

Eighty per cent of our thoughts are negative (Wax, 2019), so allow me to explain the negativity bias a bit more deeply, because it's fundamental to understanding apathy. It is our capacity to weight negative input more heavily than positive input. It's here for a good reason: to keep us out of harm's way. Throughout human history, our survival has depended on our skill at dodging danger. The brain developed systems that would make it impossible for us not to notice danger and hopefully respond to it quickly.

> The bad stuff is easier to believe. You ever notice that?
>
> **—Julia Roberts'**
> **character in**
> *Pretty Woman*

In the limbic system of your brain, there is a small and primitive emotion processor called the amygdala. According to scientists, the amygdala uses about two-thirds of its neurons to look for bad news (Jaworski, 2019). They also say that negativity has a stronger imprint on our brains than positivity. So true, right? You can have a roomful of people applauding you, but that one guy with his arms folded is the one who sticks in your brain. Some researchers assert that negative emotions have an impact close to three times stronger than positive emotions. They have also demonstrated that the brain reacts more strongly to stimuli it deems negative. There's a greater surge in electrical activity. Thus, our attitudes are more heavily influenced by bad news than good news.

The problem with negativity bias is that it is not very sophisticated and struggles in a modern world. It's a bit like being handcuffed to a two-metre-tall, musclebound, overprotective thug who's well-meaning but just a bit thick. On the rare occasion the thug is helpful, but most of the time, it misreads situations and tries to control and protect you when you don't need protection. It tells you nonsense and, frankly, can be a perpetual pain in the butt. The thug is that voice in your head that should never be said out loud, especially if it's talking to another thug. Some people externalise the thug and get angry, but in a professional context, most of us will internalise it, which is also toxic. That energy will eventually manifest in a more passive-aggressive way.

Most societies have now recognised the thug, and we choose to turn to civility rather than thuggery as a way of living together, but do not think for a second that your thug is dead. Your thug is very much alive and well. It's no wonder that if someone has just been promoted to become a manager but has no idea how to do it, their thug will try to compensate. Your thug senses danger and therefore *fee-fi-fo-fums* to life, trying to protect you. If you don't wise up to your thug, it can cause all sorts of trouble. I have learned to hug my thug and get to know it, because although its intentions are fear based, underneath all the crazy, it just seeks safety. We'll talk about the importance of safety shortly. However, untrained, your thug is an apathy-generating machine that sees others as a danger and therefore is determined to keep connection to a minimum.

> You don't see the world as it is, you see it as you are.
>
> **—Stephen Covey**

From the lack of a simple acknowledgement when passing another human being in a corridor to the heartless and controlling nature of a self-consumed founder, apathy is *everywhere* in business. Yet trust is *everything* in business. These two opposing forces do not work together. They are opposites and repel each other. It is this deadly dance I see in the workplace all the time—an insistence on trusting various shades of apathy. Instead of a steadfast desire to build trust, we accept apathy like a grotesque, worthless ornament that was bequeathed by some distant aunt. We know it's crap, but we feel compelled to pass it onto the next generation. There's a deep tug that says apathy is our sole protector. It's not. It's a lie. You've been hoodwinked. Apathy is the enemy of strong and powerful relationships. Apathy is numbing you, not nurturing you; and at work, it starts before you even sign up for the role.

Consider how you begin your relationships with a company. Imagine if you got a twelve-page contract on your wedding day. Would you be less or more excited about that future life with your newlywed? Would that bureaucratic gesture make you feel that trust was the basis of that relationship? I'm not knocking due diligence when recruiting; in fact, setting clear expectations is critical, but the contract is often the last thing to be sent to a potential employee and is usually emailed with the understanding of no negotiation (particularly for younger employees). I recently reviewed an employee contract and challenged why the word 'obey' was in the text! That word used to be in many a wedding vow, but now it's mostly obsolete. Just think if a contract was presented to you on the eve of your marriage. Suddenly, that joyous celebration becomes a soulless administrative chore. As the bells peal, some mysterious uncle you've never met before thrusts a hefty document in your face and says, 'Sign it, or the ring, the honeymoon, and the exciting life that were promised will be a pipe dream!' It's simply apathetic to do things the old way. Potential employees are looking for an onboarding experience that stands out from the competition and helps them connect to the company and its people. They don't want new employees' enthusiasm squashed before they've started.

We can do things better, and forward-thinking companies who see the importance of trust are really investing in the onboarding experience because they recognise that this sort of investment builds trust and therefore builds relationships, leading to deeper connections and consequently awesome collaborations.

'Humbug!' says apathy. Well, one study found that companies where employees were encouraged to work together sat within the 64 per cent higher portion of high-growth organisations (Coleman, 2017). Collaboration based on trust works.

A mind shift is needed to dispel the belief that we must only focus on the transactional nature of business. It's often a wonderful excuse not to invest in the transformational qualities of learning and development because the business needs another round of funding or a particular product needs to be shipped before they can think of such luxuries. That is apathy often disguised as efficiency. It's nuts because you can't outsource empathy. 'Clients do not come first, employees come first. If you take care of your employees, they'll take care of the clients': an awesome quote by Richard Branson.

> Systems and processes are essential to keep the crusade going, but they should not replace the crusade.
>
> **– Simon Sinek**

A growth mindset *always* has an intention to learn. If development opportunities are not available and your leaders are dismissing them as 'nice to haves', then they are displaying apathy and have a fixed mindset.

The crusade is more than just the basic job responsibilities and transactional elements of the working day. Think about the purpose of the manager–team member relationship:

1. To positively further the business.
2. To connect and collaborate with each individual in your team (the imperative and innate desire to positively connect and collaborate with other humans. Near impossible without trust).

We're together to work, that's *what* we're doing; but the work in itself is nowhere near enough to keep us together. *Why* we're there is way more compelling. The 'why' often needs to be fleshed out to connect us to a deep purpose, (more on that shortly) but human connection must also shine through. That definitely includes connecting with the other team members, strengthening relationships, building on those connections, questioning motives, laughing with and at each other and enjoying the tussle of the competition. Connection is the kinetic force that energises trust. Burn this into your brain. It's super important. Moreover, human connection, in my view, is nothing less than the elixir of life! Remember that the most important things in life *aren't* things!

A lack of these sorts of connections is devastating businesses and our wider lives. Read Johann Hari's book *Lost Connections* (Hari, 2018). It's a game changer. Johann has done tons of research into the importance of meaningful connection and collaboration to bring worth and value to life. He makes a compelling case about our human heritage always being centred on and in a tribe. We were surrounded by hundreds of kinsfolk who had our backs; indeed, our survival was based on being in and working with the tribe. Humans have never been the fastest or strongest, but we can work incredibly well together. These intrinsic qualities of intelligence *and* collaboration have made us the dominant species. But over time, this tribal force has diminished, and now surveys in the Western world show how we've become the loneliest and most depressed we've ever been. We've lost touch with each other; we've lost those important connections, which Johann notes are as important as food and water. It is a sense of belonging and purpose or even the basic need to be seen as somebody worthy of existence. All these things give us the motivation to create and contribute. *Lost Connections* is an invaluable read to understand the importance of human connection.

Please consider this carefully; otherwise, you'll completely miss the point of this book. Yes, we need the business. It's our shared story, but the power is not just in the work; it's around it! The work itself is lifeless without human connection.

> Human connections are deeply nurtured in the field of a shared story.
>
> **—Jean Houston**

The power is in the people who trust and collaborate. Without them, there is no business. The better the human connection is, the more the business collaborates, and great collaboration is key to success. I love this quote: 'Collaboration divides the task and multiplies the success!' (author unknown). Great managers are *amazing* collaborators and foster strong alliances and partnerships in the workplace. Vala Afshar from Salesforce said, 'We're not a team because we work together. We are a team because we respect, trust and care for each other.' Not far off from what Simon Sinek said a few pages back, right? There's a theme, my friends. Maybe these extraordinary and exceptional folks have a point.

I've worked with many incredible tech start-ups. I see amazing innovation in

> We only want to link up with people whom we like, admire, and trust ... We do not wish to join with managers who lack admirable qualities, no matter how attractive the prospects of their business. We've never succeeded in making a good deal with a bad person.
>
> **—Warren Buffett**

these businesses, but the way they 'skill up' managers of people is either non-existent or stuck in the days when Steve Jobs was a mere twinkle in his parents' eyes. Even when Jobs did get into management, his behaviour towards others was widely reported to be so belligerent that it could well have driven the Dalai Lama to a diva outburst. He certainly made a company that the world envies, but behind the scenes, his attitude could seriously stink. Believe me, that's a price a modern workforce will not pay and employment law now strictly guards against.

As a kid, I remember being envious of a boy in my class. He had no siblings; I had five. He had a big house; my house was great but not palatial, like his. He got whatever he wanted; my parents were incredibly generous, but they had to please six children, not one. I stayed at this boy's house for a sleepover one night. Never again. Whereas my house was buzzing with energy and warmth, his place was dead. The energy was cold. When his dad arrived home, I could hear him arguing in whispered tones with his wife. Dinner was a silent affair with the exception of the father criticising his son whilst winking at me. *Weird.* I couldn't wait to get back home. We often judge our insides against others' outsides. Looking at Apple's success, is it really worth stealing people's peace of mind and sense of joy to keep the boss happy? Not for me. Absolutely not.

Andy (who ran her own public relations consultancy at the time) claims to have been fired *five times* by Steve Jobs. On the first occasion, Jobs refused to pay her $35,000 that she was owed. Andy got her contract renewed only after threatening Jobs that she'd tell the business press about his 'other' side. Andy says that Jobs' behaviour 'pushed her harder',

> Steve got angry with everybody that worked with him. He threw things at people, swore at people, criticised their clothing (Pagano & Kakoyiannis, 2017). What it did to certain people, caused us to push even harder and try to be even better, but for some people it destroyed them.
>
> **—Andy Cunningham (fired by Steve Jobs five times)**

but to me, being shouted and sworn at or having stuff thrown in my direction is not a motivator for high performance. Having to threaten Jobs to get her money back and then stick around to get fired four more times does not seem like the basis of a healthy relationship.

In Andy's defence, some leaders' charisma is seductive, and we forgive their shadow side too easily, allowing the abnormal to become the norm. Steve Jobs was a genius, but in today's workplace, this behaviour is simply unacceptable. We saw this at Uber, as Travis Kalanick's behaviour hit the headlines. These leaders are not alone. There are plenty of other questionable characters in companies. I'm not suggesting that we should stifle passion at work. I'm talking about managing emotions and being able to conduct meaningful performance conversations without losing the plot or shutting down. If someone's crying their eyes out and says, 'I'm fine,' clearly, they're not fine, and their team leaders need tools to handle the complexities of human relationships. We need to connect to each other's hearts, not try and fix emotions with our heads. Knocking heads together does not increase heartfelt connection. It'll just give everyone a headache.

Many, many managers fall into the age-old trap of reacting to stress by using their IQ or simply disregarding and being indifferent to the humanity of their team members.

Settling for a life of self-imposed apathy may suit the individual, but it makes communication difficult for others. It's no surprise that those displaying apathetic traits also display some form of passive aggression. This is a toxic place where communication becomes complicated. Yes means no, and confusing messages actually inadvertently encourage apathy in others. Then there's blatant, nonchalant apathy, where a smile is a grimace. It's driven by hundreds of different things, from self-centred fear to misplaced stoicism. This saddens me. It's usually seen in men and women who have been in a business for a while. To me, they come across like a lion in a zoo that has lost the wild spark in its eyes. These people end up pacing around their territory (cage), are super difficult to manage (if you enter their cage, you may get bitten badly), and can cause untold damage to themselves, their colleagues, and therefore the business. When new team members are managed by these people, the results are often disastrous. The only thing the newbie learns is how to be successfully apathetic.

It's such a shame to hear this from experts, like Bianca McCann, the chief human resources officer at BetterWorks, who says, 'We know from research that empathy is on the decline.' Yet we know that empathy can and does successfully drive incredible results. One study from the NHS (the National Health Service in the UK) showed that higher engagement levels in employees equated to lower patient mortality rates! The study found that there were four areas that created engaged team members: engaging managers, having integrity, having a strategic narrative, and making employees feel their voices are being heard (Engage for Success, 2014). These are all developed in *The Trust Triangle* program to create the magical mixture that builds trust.

> Trust is the highest form of human motivation.
>
> —Stephen Covey

Time and again, we focus on expertise, dismissing energy and empathy. I remember sharing a stage with a renowned professor. He walked on the stage and muttered through his presentation, looking up twice. He had the enthusiasm of slug, and boy, we felt it. The energy was sucked out of the room. He completely disregarded the audience as his monosyllabic monologue trudged on for what felt like an eternity. Your intellect does not give you a 'get out of empathy' card. Your position of power at work should never mean you're allowed to offer less energy or empathy than others. Unfortunately, many managers are missing the basics and not empathically connecting with their team as well as they could. The good news is you're a human, and therefore, once you learn a few skills, this will come naturally to you. It's just a matter of focusing on the right things to become a stand-out team leader. The solution is a simple pivot.

If you've ever used a camera with autofocus, you'll know what it's like to zoom in on a particular subject. I remember trying to take a picture of a bird, but my camera kept focusing on a branch close to it. It was so frustrating. As I fumbled with the camera settings, the bird flew away. Our autofocus in the workplace isn't great. We spend our time focusing on IQ rather than EQ (emotional intelligence). We think we can solve people problems with spreadsheets and analytics.

> When you change the way you look at things, the things you look at change.
>
> **—Wayne Dyer**

In a breakthrough book *The Mindful Way through Depression* (Williams, Teasdale, Segal, & Kabat-Zinn, 2007), the authors make a powerful point about this. In a section called 'Why We Can't Problem-Solve Our Emotions', they demonstrate how we use our IQ to problem-solve many issues, but that method is disastrous to solve EQ issues. Let's unpack that a little. Our IQ wants to first define the problem, then discover the root cause and finally decide what a great solution would look like.

> There is zero correlation between IQ and emotional empathy. They're controlled by different parts of the brain.
>
> **— (Goleman, Daniel Goleman: Why aren't we more compassionate? | TED Talk, 2017)**

From that data, a plan is formed and then executed to deliver a solution. With emotions, that formula just makes everything worse! By defining the problem, we confirm the pain. By looking at the root cause, we verify the pain, and by looking at the solution, we attest to how far away we are from a solution and therefore create more pain. The authors show how *being* rather than *doing* is the answer to emotional disturbance. Empathy is being with someone rather than imposing on someone. A quick fix doesn't work and just makes matters worse. Understanding this is understanding how humans work. We're still pushing people and wondering why they push back. We try to control them and wonder why they resist. By the time we recognise that this isn't working for someone, we're sitting in their exit interview.

We need to stop trying to fill a round hole with a square peg. The round hole being humans, and the square peg being just IQ. Sure, our intelligence separates us from animals, *but so does our empathy.*

The scales have weighed far too heavily on intelligence in the workplace. I have met Harvard graduates who are absolute schmucks. I have met school dropouts who I've been mesmerised by. However, it's not an either/or. I will not ridicule intelligence in this book. For example, I want my doctors to know what they're talking about, but without empathy, they can be very dangerous.

Accountability

> **Definition: accountability**—an obligation or willingness to accept responsibility or to account for one's actions.

This particular definition mentions obligation *or* willingness. I'd replace the 'or' with 'and', as there are managers who are obliged to be accountable but lack the willingness to truly accept any responsibility. Instead of accounting for one's actions, they blame others (including their own team, by throwing them under the bus) to save themselves. Such shameful behaviour usually catches up with them.

Accountability is critical. You are in the driving seat, and yes, the conditions on the road may be made

> A smooth sea never made a good sailor.
>
> **—Franklin D Roosevelt**

difficult due to external and internal factors, *but* if you drive on with empathy, I promise that it'll be a fulfilling ride!

Remember what I'm *not* looking for. I don't want a manager who gets off on power and control. It's a classic apathy move to be 'apart from' rather than 'a part of' a team. This demonstrates the necessity to practise shared leadership to keep your feet on the ground. More on this methodology later.

Be in the team and not above it. Needless to say, I'm not looking for a manager who kisses up, kicks down, or blames the top, the bottom, and everyone in between in a bid to divert attention away from their woeful performance. It's not about having the power to control people; it's about unleashing people power!

Too many leaders are keen to promote people into management without giving them the tools to prosper, and some new managers are keen to take the pay increase but not the responsibility. As Gandhi said, 'Be the change.' That first requires making a choice. The responsibility for your success is *yours*. A significant number of people *say* they want change in their lives but *do* nothing, and others go in all guns blazing and then give up. Then there are others who are consistently determined to give something (like this program) a real go. The latter attitude will normally find success.

> Most people do not really want freedom, because freedom involves responsibility, and most people are frightened of responsibility.
>
> **—Sigmund Freud**

Freud focused on the fear of change. I remember watching a documentary about a lion that had lived in captivity all its life and was being freed into the open plains of Africa. After all the rehab required to prepare this majestic animal for the wild, the moment came when the cage was delivered to some remote place in the savannah. The cameras rolled as the cage was opened, and the handlers ran to safety, ready for the lion to launch itself out of the constraints of the cage and gallop off into the sunset. Nothing happened. The lion refused to budge. He put a paw out occasionally but wouldn't move. The presenter pondered whether the lion was, in fact, fearful of the prospect of this new life. It was a reasonable assumption to make. Eventually, he was coaxed out with food (it works for me), and off he tentatively went into the wild. If you want to be the king of the jungle, you have to take those steps into the unknown.

It's really down to you. Here's some more inspiration:

> The price of greatness is responsibility.
>
> **—Winston Churchill**

The more I researched, the more I found the same message, over and over again:

This calling, from some of the greatest minds who have ever lived, shows us that a passive attitude simply will not do. If you want to be a remarkable manager, it comes at a price. That price is action and your responsibility to persevere with this program, no matter what.

> Enough of the 'poor me', or 'they were just lucky' or any other excuses. 'Responsibility finds a way. Irresponsibility makes excuses!
>
> **—Gene Bedley**

> Liberty means responsibility. That's why most men dread it.
>
> **—George Bernard Shaw**

So, come on. Let's get into transformation territory. Change requires more than just thinking. I've never just thought myself better. Success in the context of *The Trust Triangle* comes from a three-pronged approach:

1. Learn it—digest the information.
2. Live it—consistently apply it to your business practice.
3. Lend it—you've only learned a lesson if you can pass it on to someone else.

I'll show you how to do it so you can then apply it. This book introduces you to tools, tips, and techniques that can truly revolutionise the way you manage people if you work them into your life.

Tools: Trust

> I have been impressed with the urgency of doing. Knowing is not enough; we must apply. Being willing is not enough; we must do.
>
> **—Leonardo da Vinci**

1. Take a blank piece of A4 and create two columns. Think of someone at work (or someone you've worked with in the past) who you really trust. Write down their qualities. In the other column, think about someone at work you really don't trust. Write down the characteristics that made you distrust them. The trust column will give you a list of brilliant attributes of a great manager. You don't need a dictionary definition of a good manager anymore. You've just written it! Are you truly practicing what you admire? If not, why not?

2. Learn to embrace and get to know your thug—your negative bias. Do not dismiss it or hide it from yourself and others. Professor Steve Peters calls the thug a 'chimp' in his awesome book *The Chimp Paradox*. Please read it.

3. Get a journal and write down your challenges and successes.

THE BACKDROP

Core Concerns

The bottom line is this: we have a default inclination towards our negativity bias, and with little or no emotional intelligence, apathy is our natural impulse and feels a lot easier than reaching out empathically to ourselves and others. It's not until we enter the workforce that this under-exercised muscle (EQ) really shows itself. Look at the sickness rate; it's no surprise that stress beats any other illness as the reason most of us are off work. And where do you think stress comes from? Simply, it's the result of people who don't know how to manage themselves or relationships at work. I see it every day: professionals not caring about their colleagues' limits and crashing through other people's boundaries or lack of boundaries. It's blatant apathy. Or it's individuals not dealing with emotional-health issues. As in society, there are *a lot* of emotionally scarred human beings who populate the workforce, with untreated emotional wounds often badly hidden. These people shut up or shut down to protect themselves, but you can't collaborate with

> If you don't heal what hurt you, you'll bleed on people who didn't cut you.
>
> **—Author unknown**

someone through triple-glazed apathy. It's only trust that can bring down defences and start the process of humans courageously connecting.

Some forward-thinking employers see this and are now offering free therapy to their staff. Now, wait a second. Think about your response to the therapy sentence you've just read. Is your response apathetic or empathic? For example, 'The workplace is no place for this therapy mumbo jumbo!' or 'Makes sense, tell me more.' Come on, friends. Wake up. You are human. The brilliant book *The Primal Wound* (Firman & Gila, 1997) says, 'At the deepest level, human beings are relational.' This means we learn and depend on each other! It goes on to say, 'The human spirit arises and develops via the nurture of empathic relationships.' By ignoring this most important and profound truth, we actually compound the problem of apathy, making others feel a sense of what the book calls 'non-being'. This means being treated less than human, a thing, an 'it' instead of an amazing being made from the frickin' stars! 'Professional' facades that promise so much are actually poison to any chance of true connection. This is because, by their very nature, they are traditionally distant, self-focused and dismissive. These are all ingredients for poor relationships and therefore a foundation for distrust.

Take a step back and look at life beyond the workplace. We are dealing with a world steeped in fear and therefore apathy. The twenty-four-hour news machine manufactures a constant flow of bad news to feed our ravenous negativity bias. It's basically fear porn and we can't get enough of it. Unfortunately, it conditions us to see the world as a scary place. Emotional contagion means fear perpetuates fear, creating a world of catastrophic extremes: a binary black-and-white place. You are either a friend or a foe. Anyone not in the inner circle of our lives (the majority of the human race) is a foe! Therefore, we become apathetic (detached, dismissive, and disinterested) to those not close to us. We stock up like we are preparing for war, with greed proliferating as a way to defend and protect us from this supposed 'dreadful' place and unseen enemy. A bigger car with blacked-out windows and a house with high fences are our goals, and the lottery is the only hope.

> Just because someone's in a gilded cage, doesn't make them a happy bird.
>
> **—Author unknown**

Please don't judge someone else's outsides by your insides. It's not a fair trade. Striving for 'stuff' will never fill the gap that human connection can and does appease. Yet we turn away from connection and eat (we're the heaviest we've ever been), drink, drug, smoke, gamble, or work harder to dampen that numbing drum of doom and despair. Wow, this is depressing (the Western world has never been so depressed) (WHO, 2018). Can you see where apathy comes from? Is it any wonder that apathy is so distinct in life and therefore in the workplace? And for most of us, our solution is to isolate more and only 'relate' superficially through social media. We crave a deeper connection and answer that call with a Photoshopped Instagram of ourselves. It's like eating gravy all our lives, desperately seeking a proper meal.

> The enemy is fear. We think it is hate but it is fear.
>
> **—Ghandi**

The other response to all of this is control. 'If only people did it the way we said, the world would be a better place.' However, the result is that life gets harder the more we try to control it. 'Me, me, me' emerges (self-centred fear), and a separation is created when it's a 'me first, screw you' world of work. There is no place for empathy in a company where meetings are like some gladiatorial ego contest rather than a productive grouping of great minds and hearts, where collaboration is a primary principle to achieve something special together.

You can be apathetic to a microwave, but humans do not go 'ding' after two minutes. We are not machines, and when treated like them, humans react to apathy with apathy, hence the proliferation of this in the professional and wider world.

Human beings are way more complex than a widget that can be turned on and off. I remember a story about a heart surgeon who went to get his car serviced. As the mechanic opened the bonnet, he said, 'We basically do the same thing. I lift the bonnet. You open up a body. We both clean out any blockages, fix a few valves, close the bonnet, and off they go.'

The surgeon considered what the mechanic had said and replied, 'There is one major difference, though.' The mechanic listened carefully as the surgeon continued: 'Try changing the valves in a car whilst the engine is still running!' Humans are not appliances that can be unplugged. Overcoming the tide of self-centred fear and the detritus of apathy that washes up in the workplace is the biggest challenge for team leaders.

Humans Are Not Machines

The industrial revolution helped us to mass-produce things, but the workforce also became 'things' that were lost in an almighty and emotionally bleak machine. They clocked in, designed things, made things, counted things, and then clocked out. The digital revolution came along and saw the machine get substantially smaller, but it still required humans. However, this generation of humans wasn't so happy just being 'things'. Today's workforce is pushing back even more, and experts like Seth Godin are now calling this age the 'connection economy' (Visceral Business, 2013). Employees want to understand their purpose and what part they play in an organisation. They don't want to be treated as 'non-beings'. They want to feel trusted, valued, and supported, but many at the top persist in imposing ridiculous control or reckless autonomy. The result is a passively less compliant workforce than that of previous generations. Instead of visually putting down their tools, they covertly put down their brains, massively damaging productivity. The more leaders push, the more the workers are pushing back. Thankfully, the winds of change are blowing, and some companies see this and are now capitalising on the real power of people, which is proving to be way more profitable than just industrial people power. You can do this too by implementing *The Trust Triangle* at work.

When ego control stops and heart collaboration starts, the 'human revolution' shows itself like the first rains on a parched plain. People come alive like dormant seeds and take root in organisations. Heart connection flourishes, and they start to care because leaders and managers care. The timewasters run for shelter as the real professionals burst into life, reinvigorated to make a genuine difference.

Apathy shows itself at the macro level as well. Cultures of countries perpetuate the myth that it's OK to disregard the human in the being. Empathy is a universal trait in all of us, no matter where we come from, so I'm not convinced that we should somehow 'let off' apathy because it's cultural. Although you'll soon discover that empathy is a choice, that choice defines us. Whether that choice is to be civil or not separates us from the animal kingdom.

We still have a long way to go, and this book aims to equip leaders of people, whether a founder, chief executive, or new manager starting their career, to stop seeing team members as things and start embracing them as humans.

Empathy Is a Choice

The amazing Brené Brown has studied human connection (please read her books) and says, 'Empathy is a choice, a vulnerable choice, because in order to connect with you I have to connect with something inside myself that knows that feeling' (The RSA, 2013).

Please burn this into your brain: *empathy is a choice* because of our ingrained bias is towards apathy. Leaning into empathy is a choice and a challenge. Please understand that I am not saying we are heartless thugs before we make this choice. Of course, we display empathy, but as professionals, we're inconsistent for many reasons, from being time starved to feeling that empathy is incompatible with our current work cultures. It's time to change! The evidence is in, and the pathway is now mapped out for you in the book.

I'm calling on you to consistently demonstrate empathy at work. We need to make a genuine, conscious choice towards empathy, and put it into action to make it a reality in our businesses. This is the core of my teachings. Conscious means awake and aware: a mindful embracing of empathy at every turn. This is simple but not easy. Apathy is a default (remember the negativity bias). It's the easy option. 'They' or 'it' is somebody else's problem. Why do you think team members disregard what their 'boss' tells them? It's obvious to me: the boss is disregarding them, and they are simply reacting—I mean literally re-acting.

It's time to realign: we rise by lifting others up, not by standing on them.

You may have thought of empathy as being your ultimate weakness. Mistake, big mistake. It is, in fact, your greatest strength. Brené Brown has found that empathy is a choice and supports this by saying it is a 'vulnerable choice' (The RSA, 2013). But there is no place for vulnerability in a culture of fear. True vulnerability comes from courage; it's not some non-critical 'soft skill'.

Soft Is Hard

Although soft and hard skills mainly refer to how easy they are to measure, there is another definition that has become synonymous with soft skills. After the horrors of World War Two, many men who returned home chose to bury deep inside the atrocious scenes they witnessed. It was seen as having a 'stiff upper lip'. This attitude made sense on the battlefield but not in business, but generation after generation, this literal heartbreaking behaviour has become the norm. Day in, day out, we salute apathy and squash empathy, denying the wholeness of our humanity.

Back in the day, and in some quarters to this day, men in particular were seen as 'soft' if they were understanding of their own and others' emotions. Women were seen as weak for their ability to empathise. We now know this is nonsense, and certain emotions cannot be successfully 'turned off'. Brené Brown's research found that 'we cannot selectively numb emotions. When we numb the painful emotions, we numb the positive emotions' (The RSA, 2013).

So, when we numb pain, we numb joy. By denying our humanness we are disregarding 50 per cent of who we intrinsically are. In the old days, those with stiff upper lips were determined to disconnect from all emotion, and this is the way lots of managers, and indeed many professionals still handle their work environment today. They try to turn their humanness down to a low setting and detach. The problem is, it doesn't work. Sure, you can manage emotions (that's what EQ is), but a team leader unskilled in EQ who walks through the work door and literally stops caring is someone I don't want to be managed by. Do you?

Ban the Word 'Boss'

I remember sitting opposite a potential client, a leader of a large organisation. Before we started, he gave me a crushing handshake and took a large gulp of coffee, revealing his cufflinks. One cufflink was scribed with, 'I am the boss', and the other said 'I'm never wrong.' I pointed them out, thinking he'd tell me a funny and hopefully embarrassing story. Wrong! He was super proud of them and said, 'I got these from some ex-colleagues who know how I tick.' In our discussions, it emerged that the biggest problem (and I see it all the time with C-suite) was that he felt his reports needed to build trust, but he didn't. He was confident he'd ticked that box many years previous. He was clearly too important and experienced to need such a program. I find this part of my job to be incredibly challenging sometimes. Over and over again, I experience the worst managers being at the top of the organisation. Remember: leaders still manage people, but they regularly miss 121s because they have something more 'important' to do. They don't turn up to trainings, set flimsy expectations by making all kinds of misguided assumptions about their team, and often over-reward themselves. However, unless they're narcissists or sociopaths, deep down, they know they're on thin ice. They're simply deluding themselves, and they know it. Great leaders love to learn with their team, fess up when they mess up, and spend quality time with their direct reports.

We need to stop playing 'boss'. Seriously, ban that awful, outdated, control-freaky word. Recoil from it as if you've been insulted if anybody calls you their 'boss'. It completely disempowers your team members and their responsibilities. Yes, your decisions will be more macro, but they need to lead too. I want them to step up and become truly accountable for their part in the organisation. Their decisions, though micro, must be encouraged. You want your team members to own their roles and responsibilities. I'm a fan of distributed or shared leadership. In this modality, everyone in the business takes responsibility for their role and is accountable, as opposed to than the normal 'leader-subordinate' roles, which encourage subservience and a parent-child relationship. I know leaders who are called 'work mums' or 'work dads'. Stop it! I want to encourage a workplace full of lions, not sheep.

Sure, there are times when we just need to deliver to get stuff out of the door. But empowered employees who own their work and are prepared to be accountable for their workflow are way more engaged than 'sheep' waiting to be fed and then blaming the grass.

The basic tenets of distributed or shared leadership are these:

- Acknowledging that all tasks are important, just some are macro, others are micro.

- Empowering team members through mutual and united accountability.
- Accepting that those closest to the problem are the most motivated to solve it.
- Being open to genuine participative decision making. Two minds are better than one.
- Freedom within a framework (autonomy only with accountability).

The Trust Triangle methodology encourages autonomy. But autonomy can only come into fruition with genuine accountability. I love Dan Pink's work, and in his book *Drive* (Pink, Drive : The Surprising Truth About What Motivates Us, 2011), which I refer to more later, he clearly articulates the need for professionals to have autonomy: 'Control leads to compliance. Autonomy leads to engagement.'

You are *not* their boss, especially those new to the workplace. They have just managed to jump from the parental nest and survive their professors at university. The tug of resistance you will sense from younger team members is the desire for autonomy. Your role is to get them there. You are their support, advocate, mentor, and confidant. You are not their owner, whip, or adversary. You lead to serve them. And don't worry—we don't just give folks the keys to the kingdom. As mentioned, autonomy must come with accountability, and that's what *The Trust Triangle* will manifest.

The Peter Principle

I love the Peter principle; it's super helpful for understanding that current skills don't necessarily prepare you for future roles.

Think of the prospect of a promotion. The Peter principle asserts that just because you're excelling in your current role, that doesn't mean you'll have the skills or attitude to succeed in the next one.

Like a team member who is awesome technically. Their emotional intelligence may not be conducive to people management. They'll offer autonomy with no accountability and avoid difficult conversations. They'll not have the skills to coach and mentor or understand how to set clear expectations. The principle talks about employees reaching their level of incompetence. Basically, promoted to a role they cannot competently cope with.

The Peter Principle was written by Laurence J. Peter (Laurence & Hull, 1994), who says, 'My analysis of hundreds of cases of occupational incompetence led me to formulate The Peter Principle: In a hierarchy every employee tends to rise to his level of incompetence.'

An in-depth study was carried out with data on sales teams from 214 firms, 53,000 workers, and 1,500 promotions, and it provided enough information to evaluate what happened to a team once a successful salesperson was promoted into the role of team leader (Wagner, 2018). The research showed that the best salespeople were more likely to be promoted, but they turned out to be the worst managers. The better they had been in sales, the worse their teams performed. What's more, people were not promoted for behaviour that might be correlated with managerial ability—in particular, those who collaborated with others were not rewarded for doing so. What mattered? Only their sales figures.

For me, the Peter principle confirms my long-held view that even though being promoted to the role of a people manager probably means you were awesome in your last role, it doesn't mean you will have the skills to lead a team. This should be a sharp wake-up call for anyone seeking a long career. Let's make sure this promotion is not your last one!

Tools: The Backdrop

- Ban the word 'boss'.
- Start applying the tenets of shared leadership.
- Become more conscious. Download a mindfulness app and start practicing to become mindful of your apathy versus empathy responses. Mindfulness is something I will discuss in detail later. I want you to start practicing this amazing technique every day. At the moment, you're probably spending an inordinate amount of time triaging distractions and wallowing in the fears of the past or the future. Mindfulness helps build your attention muscles and turn your attention where you wish rather than to any whim.

THE TRUST TRIANGLE

I've met deranged ones, committed ones, should-be committed ones, left-for-dead ones, OK ones, and really good ones. Team leaders come in all shades of mental health and emotional wellbeing. They are the number one reason why a team member will leave a company and the number-one reason why another will be turbo engaged, the latter making the business more money while having a great time. You've probably come across the old adage that people don't leave their job; they leave their manager. I have read more research than is healthy on this subject, and managers are getting a beating from all corners. Among other things, you're 'crap', 'callous', 'carefree', 'compulsive', 'controlling', and 'cowardly'. Remember, I don't blame managers; I blame apathy. Just google 'train my manager'. Last time I looked, there were 649,000,000 results!

People often become managers because they're technically competent in the area of business they're in. For example, a developer who has produced brilliant code and been in the business for a while will be considered for promotion to manager, but as I hope you now understand, the skills required for managing people are different to coding.

Before we get to *The Trust Triangle*, I want to point out a few insights. Firstly, the reason for the relationship, and then personal perspectives.

Reason for Relationship

This book is all about how to practically instil trust, and there are some tactics I see that are counterproductive. Please don't foster a relationship with your team members that's based on the business being the enemy. After all, it's the reason you're together. The business has higher merit in the context of this relationship, as it is the instigator of and motivator for you both being together. There may well come a time when you have to make decisions regarding your team members that demonstrate this, from having a difficult performance conversation to redundancy. However, I suggest that this need not be a power play. It's understanding that you both have a role to play within the business, not out of the business looking in. If you're bitching about the business as a way to motivate your team, you're bound for failure! It's not us and them, managers are us *and* them.

> Leaders who don't listen will eventually be surrounded by people who have nothing to say.
>
> **—Andy Stanley**

The next relationship to avoid is you (the manager) and the business working in cahoots and not sharing with the team members. Sure, there are some confidences that are kept away from all eyes (like other team members' private conversations with the people team or extremely sensitive data about the business), but I suggest that most stuff in the business could be shared more widely. People become cautious around too much secrecy and always imagine the worst (remember the negativity bias) and it feeds psychological unsafety. It also gives the impression that you are more special than them. So, avoid the manager and business versus the team members.

Finally, the weirdest relationship (and it's not that uncommon) is the one where the business and the team members are in cahoots against the manager. 'I know Terry is difficult and can get very angry,' says the HR manager to the team member, 'but he's your manager, and that's that. If he shouts at you again, come and see me and I'll do nothing.' Of course, this is apathy personified. A manager being allowed to act inappropriately but being accepted in the business for whatever reason. Tragic.

Please make sure there is a rounded relationship that benefits all parties.

Personal Perspectives

The weight you place on your personal perspectives will determine how you deal with your day. Remember, you don't see the world as it is—you see the world as you are! This is basically how you see the world from your point of view, either consciously or not.

Frances Frei is a Harvard professor and an expert on trust. In an awesome TED Talk on this subject (Frei, 2018), she explains the three components that build trust. Please watch it—she's fantastic! Clear logic, authenticity and empathy. I use different words, but in essence, they mean the same in the context of the workplace:

- Expertise (logic)—what you do
- Energy (authenticity)—how you do it
- Empathy—who you do it with

I overheard a couple walking behind me the other day, discussing someone with an 'amazing CV'. I heard one reel off the many academic achievements this person has, as well as the fantastic experience she will be accumulating from her (soon to be starting) first position. I didn't hear them speak about her character or her ability to collaborate. Traditionally, we have put far too much emphasis on 'expertise' in the workplace, so much so that we accept intolerable attitudes and even sociopathic tendencies because someone went to a top university or has an extraordinary skill. The good news is that a better balance is being taken more and more seriously as energy and empathy are now being given equal status with expertise. Frankly, I find it odd that empathy was ever pushed aside when you think that the primary concern in business is to solve another person's problem. How do you do that without empathy?

My core point here is this: we try to run a business from the level of our individual perspective, but everyone has a different view. Sure, managers have different styles; we're all unique, BUT what has been lacking is an agreed road map for managers to build trust and therefore deliver what's been promised. *The Trust Triangle* gives you that agreed road map.

Imagine if your salespeople each used different methodologies; it would be chaos. Sales teams flourish when they have an agreed-upon modus operandi with enough flexibility for personalities to shine through.

Everyone's perspectives are different but cracking the code for building trust with clear and simple directions has been elusive. Until now.

To the focus of this book: *The Trust Triangle*. There are three domains, and each domain has three disciplines. These nine disciplines are your practical anchors needed to develop trust in the workplace and become an awesome team leader. People managers need people skills, and these nine disciplines come up time and time again as clear motivators to build trust.

The Trust Triangle

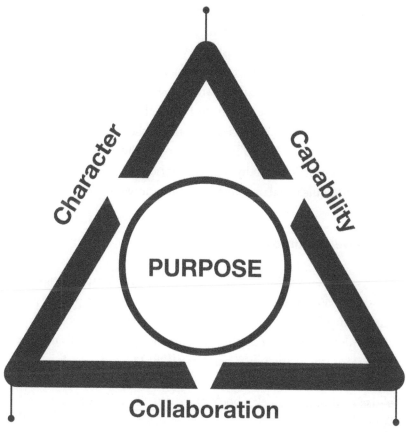

Energy
- Psychological Safety
- Seeks Deeper Connection
- Celebrates Success

Character

Capability

PURPOSE

Collaboration

Empathy
- Emotional Intelligence
- Contextualises Communication
- Coaches and Mentors

Expertise
- Sets Clear Expectations
- Evidence Based
- Results Driven

Trust is born from these three domains: empathy, energy, and expertise. As I have unapologetically reinforced, we dismiss emotional intelligence (EQ) for expertise (IQ). When this happens, our energy changes, and we become people pleasers, procrastinators, performers, and panderers. The Trust Triangle brings real balance to any professional relationship.

Of course, expertise is important at work. However, as you counterbalance that with empathy, fake energy recedes, and a genuine curiosity and interest in the other party drives a deeper connection and better relationships. A good way to look at *The Trust Triangle* is to imagine a butcher's scales. The left pan is the empathy domain which seeks to understand. The expertise domain is the right pan and seeks to be understood while the energy domain is the beam that holds the scales together. It allows the balance (the energy) to take place, and, as you'll soon discover, the energy domain is basically Maslow's hierarchy of needs (abridged). *The Trust Triangle* brings an exquisite balance to relationships at work.

The Power of Purpose

As you can see in *The Trust Triangle*, it has 'purpose' right in the centre. Purpose matters. Studies have found that people with purpose live 15 per cent longer than those who don't. Purpose-driven companies are 40 per cent better at retaining their staff and they outperform the market by 7 per cent (IDEO U, n.d.).

If you really want to understand the power of purpose, then please read Simon Sinek's book *Start with Why* (Sinek, Start with Why: How Great Leaders Inspire Everyone to Take Action, 2011), and check out his TED talk about the golden circle (TED, Simon Sinek: How Great Leaders Inspire Action | TED Talk, 2009). Simon is a master at this, so take his advice, and first consider why the business exists before you move onto the what and how. Businesses are about making money, but Simon says that's the *result* of working our purpose and not the 'why'.

Ralph Waldo Emerson said, 'The purpose of life is not to be happy. It is to be useful, to be honourable, to be compassionate, to have it make some difference that you have lived and lived well.' Ralph is right, so make sure your team members understand the purpose behind their usefulness, and you'll see an upwards drive in performance.

In an eye-opening report by PwC called 'Putting Purpose to Work' (PwC, n.d.), the authors noted, 'While business leaders prioritise the commercial value of purpose, employees see purpose as a way to bring meaning to their work and understand the contributions they are making to the company, as well as society.'

And here's what they found:

Value of purpose in the workplace	Employees	Business leaders
Meaning in day-to-day work	83%	52%
Strong sense of community	56%	25%
Reputation for growth and innovation	30%	72%

Here it is in black and white, a significant disconnect regarding what purpose is depending on where you sit in the hierarchy. Therefore, many businesses are creating purpose statements based on what leaders think and are completely missing the point for those on the shop floor. Please make sure that 'the why' makes sense for all your employees; it should not be something that leadership owns and employees ignore.

Without a clear purpose, *The Trust Triangle* is like a rudderless ship. Please make sure you agree and then anchor your purpose to everything you do. It's more important than ever to get this right, as the PwC report also found that millennials are five times more likely to stay in a business when they have a strong connection to their employer's purpose.

I do not claim to be an expert in this area and businesses need to invest proper resource into finding their purpose if it's not clear or not owned by everyone. If your employer's purpose is weak, then please share with the leadership how imperative purpose is to the success of its goals.

Let's dive a little deeper into what *The Trust Triangle* domains mean and the skills you'll develop.

EMPATHY: To understand

Emotional Intelligence

- Self-awareness and awareness of others.
- Significantly better relationships.
- Improved resilience.
- Increased influence and impact.
- Consistency with the awareness of your negativity bias.

Contextualises Communication

- Don't just show up and throw up. Make sure you craft any conversation for the audience you're in front of. One size does not fit all. You will see this when you manage a team. Everyone is unique, and so is the way they see the world.
- Great communication is key. Hold scheduled (and try your best not to cancel) fortnightly 121s with your team members.
- Have daily five- to ten-minute stand-ups so everyone knows the plans for the day.

- Conflict is inevitable in a successful workplace, but combat is optional. Learn the skill of having meaningful conversations using constructive feedback techniques.
- As you become a more established manager, your communication skills will be called on more and more for the likes of company presentations and leadership briefings. Learn this skill sooner rather than later.

Coaches and Mentors

- Encourage a learning culture to spark a growth mindset.
- Spend time with your team members using coaching techniques, such as GROW.
- Mentor your team members to help develop and reach their goals.
- Make sure you're nurturing authentic selves and not fake facades.
- Encourage open chats about wellbeing, and don't forget to look after yourself.

ENERGY: Maslow's Hierarchy of Needs (abridged)

Psychological Safety

- Discourage a default culture of negativity and fear.
- Value people as much as process. Organisations are a collection of humans working for a common purpose.
- Encourage a business where we confront negative behavior.
- Discover the power of intrinsic motivation compared with the flimsier extrinsic motivators at work.

Seeks Deeper Connection

- You can gain a richer understanding of your colleagues by connecting more deeply and therefore collaborating like an 'A' player.
- You don't know everything. Keep an open mind rather than a fixed mindset.
- Big egos have little ears! Great collaborators listen—I mean, really listen.

Celebrates Success

- Great team members thank each other for their work.
- Leaders regularly offer praise both personally and on a bigger stage.
- An attitude of gratitude is inspired. It's difficult to be grateful and unhappy.
- Negativity bias is countered.

EXPERTISE: To be understood

Sets Clear Expectations

- Take deliberate action towards a considered and super-clear goal.
- Emphasise collaboration, not control.
- Agree on expectations, do not impose them.
- Set clear expectations as the root of awesome delegation.
- Nurture psychological safety so team members feel OK about asking silly questions.

Evidence Based

- Visual indicators that show progress.
- Decisions based on empirical data, not a whim. Leaders need data to understand whether or not their strategy is working.
- What is your team achieving? It's imperative to be able to clearly demonstrate with data, not hearsay. Performance management systems are not micromanagement. It's where you can see real progress and problems as well as see areas where we can celebrate success or challenge.
- Awesome autonomy grows from sincere accountability. You need to be accountable partners, not taskmasters. Being evidence-based demonstrates that you are actually doing what was agreed on.

Results Driven

- If setting clear expectations is the root of delegation, this is the branch where fruit is borne.
- Set clear daily, weekly and monthly horizons that need to be met. You'll be judged on what your team produces, not what you say they'll produce. Please, stand and deliver! We expect everyone to be 'busy', but what are you delivering?
- Prioritise. This skill develops accountability and encourages autonomy. Map out the priorities *and* consistently munch on the smaller tasks.
- Leaders need to see results, and team members need to see they're making an impact.

- You and your team members produce weekly reports to clarify what has been achieved.
- An important outcome of this discipline is the ability for team members to work autonomously as a result of clear expectations that are evidence-based.

Once clear expectations are set, we can focus on delivery and not on someone turning up five minutes late. The reason businesses are wary of flexible working is that *they* fail to set clear expectations and delivery targets on quantity and quality, and their reporting (evidence based) is woeful and inconsistent.

A great trust triangle needs the right capabilities and good character traits to give the net result of trust which fuels genuine collaboration. Ego-fuelled control disappears, and connection blossoms. If you've ever seen two people or a team working *The Trust Triangle* way, you'll know how awesome it is. However, it only works if you work it.

Be habitual about using *The Trust Triangle* so the domains become second nature. According to a study by UCL it takes sixty-six days to form a habit (UCL, 2009), so keep on keeping on. Learn this stuff, then live it. The best way to create new habits is to get right on and create them. If you cannot chronicle change in each of the domains of *The Trust Triangle* by the end of this book, then you need to reflect on whether this has been a talking shop rather than a chance for change and genuine growth. There is a checklist for change at the end of the book to help you execute rather than procrastinate.

4

EMPATHY

The first domain is *empathy.* Leaders need to have a deep understanding of what their team members are going through. I hope I have made a compelling

> All advocacy is, at its core, an exercise in empathy.
>
> **—Samantha Power**

case up to this point for you to take empathy seriously. Basically, how can you empower others if you don't know what is blocking them?

Empathy in an organisation is like the current in a river. I have walked into companies where the whiff of stagnant water soon becomes apparent. Rivers effortlessly move many tons of water but try doing it manually! The saddest observation is when I meet a professional in a team who gets the importance of empathy and connection but is hopelessly thrashing about in a pond, trying to give it some movement. Connection does not work unless two parties take part. It's like a chain—it needs to be coupled for it to be a chain. Apathy is the hacksaw to connection. An uncoupled team is not a team. Empathy is the number-one way to create connection. Empathy is not passive and needs action and commitment. It requires you!

Most experts agree on three common types of empathy:

- **Cognitive empathy.** The ability to be a good perspective taker. In MBTI (The Myers-Briggs Company, n.d.), strong 'Ts' (thinkers and logically minded individuals) will be more likely to demonstrate cognitive empathy. They do 'feel' but prefer a more objective view of the world.
- **Emotional empathy.** Rescuers reside here—they are able to truly stand in someone else's shoes but are not great at managing their own emotions. Their boundaries are not always robust, either. They love to give advice, but most folks don't really want advice; they just need to be truly heard.
- **Compassionate empathy.** These people can also walk in someone else's shoes but understand that they can't necessarily 'fix' someone. They are available and will do their best to help, within certain bounds.

So, strive for compassionate empathy. Remain mindful to listen and stay curious without judgment or the need to rescue. Understand what you can and can't do. Most importantly, be really present with someone. Lots of professionals struggle with this. They love to 'do' rather than 'be'.

'What can I do Matthew?' they ask in class. Empathy is more about being with someone rather than doing stuff with them. That's why 121s are so important. I'll describe a narrative on 121s shortly.

Empathy is the domain that most businesspeople have sorely neglected. That's why it's first. The problem is clear: managers are seeking to be understood (expertise domain) but not to understand (empathy domain). Hence why balance is necessary. (Remember the butcher's scales analogy).

The ability to empathise is crucial in all areas of business. From understanding the needs of a potential client to hiring a new team member, the curiosity to understand and connect is critical. When dealing with any sentient being, the right choice is empathy, every time. Even if you're firing someone, done right, it's an empathic response. They are perhaps not right for the environment, the team, or the job itself. Letting people go not only benefits the business but can also be the best decision for the individual. I've seen people flourish in different environments. So, get this: your culture is not for everyone! It is not the most awesome or the most awful place in the world. For some people, the work environment at your place is really not their scene and they need to find their tribe rather than be stuck in your culture, which just isn't for them. Encouraging that right choice *is* empathy.

Do not be fooled into thinking that an empathic response is about being sweet, winsome, or nice. In the workplace, managers or leaders who feel they're too nice and think they need to harden up believe that the only way to do so is to be more apathetic. What they haven't realised is that they're already being apathetic with niceness. Kim Scott, in her wonderful book *Radical Candor* (Scott, 2018), would place those people in a quadrant called 'ruinous empathy'. Basically, they care too much to tell their team members the truth. My response is they probably don't really care nearly as much as they think they do. If they did, they'd at least explore radical candour: the ability to care personally and challenge directly. What they're actually portraying is a toxic mixture of inner apathy and misplaced sympathy. They fall into some weird passive-aggressive pattern when trying to handle unacceptable behaviour. What happens? They get to boiling point and find that it's tough to do a U-turn, or they suddenly become difficult with the team member, who reacts with confusion at the manager's sudden mood swing. This behaviour is apathy. This is not nice; it's cruel. The team member ends up bewildered and even more disengaged. One study found that 31 per cent of managers gave a team member the silent treatment. Let's stop dismissing empathy as being nice. Being clear with someone about expectations and understanding their roadblocks is not always sweet, but it need not be bitter either.

How on earth can you expect to build trust from a place of disconnection and dishonesty? You devalue your integrity, and you're not actually helping the team member, yourself, or the business. In the 'contextualises communication' discipline, I'll take you through how to have tricky conversations.

It's important we aim our cannons to encourage our team members to feel trusted, valued, and supported. Please note that trust and a sense of being valued can take time to build, so leaders can fall into the trap of preferring a gratuitous act of generosity when they feel the workplace is at a low point rather than offering a more sustainable long-term solution. That's why this book does not aim to make a fellow professional particularly 'happy'. I love fun and a good laugh, but that vibe is always fleeting. I'm looking for something more durable, and all the evidence points to three areas for continual employee satisfaction: trusted, valued, and supported.

Infantilising the workplace is not empathic. I remember meeting an HR manager who was very pleased to report that he'd bought the team some Lego! He'd become 'daddy' rather than manager. Infantilising the workplace is not empathic. I love bright colours and beanbags, but friends, let's get serious about your team's well-being. Lego and cake are fab, but in order to have an effective team, please stop treating them like children and aim for an adult-to-adult relationship.

The **EMPATHY DOMAIN** covers three disciplines:

Emotional Intelligence
Contextualises Communication
Coaches and Mentors

Emotional Intelligence

A snake entered a hardware store. As he slithered around, he accidentally cut himself on a saw. Angry, the snake swiftly turned and bit the saw. By doing so, he seriously lacerated his mouth. Thinking that the saw was attacking him, he decided to coil around the saw, attempting to suffocate it with his entire body. The more it hurt, the more he squeezed, finally shaking the saw with all his strength to kill it. Unfortunately, the snake died of horrific injuries. Sometimes we react in anger, but all we're doing is just hurting ourselves.

I have seen an experienced journalist kick a printer and a highly intelligent founder lose his temper without understanding the whole story. So, no matter how big your IQ is, when you're managing others, you must hone your EQ.

To keep it simple, imagine EQ as heart and IQ as head. Human beings are emotional—fact—but feelings aren't always facts, and that's where it gets tricky. Remember the three basic domains for building trust. Only expertise is based on IQ; the other two (energy and empathy) are based on your EQ.

If the only thing you gain from this book is increased emotional intelligence, I'll be as happy as a fiancée at the proposal when the diamond ring is presented and she wholeheartedly accepts. Emotional intelligence in the workplace is rare but as precious as diamonds. My daily work revolves around showing people their personal diamond mine. Remember diamonds are not found as you see them in the shops. They're covered in muck. My job is to reveal your diamond in the rough.

I came across a study from PepsiCo showing that company units headed by managers with well-developed EQs outperformed yearly revenue targets by 15–20 per cent (Trotta, 2018). The exact opposite was true for managers with underdeveloped EQs. Yet, time and time again, I see professionals with a good or great IQ but a poorly developed EQ. This is a recipe for disaster as they are managing humans, not vacuum cleaners.

We are dealing with humans, who can be as neurotic and nasty as they can be outstanding and innovative. People are complex. In some research about different types of problems, researchers at York University in Canada (Glouberman & Zimmerman, 2002) noted that problems generally fall into three categories:

1. **Simple problems** like following a recipe. Once you've overcome some basic issues around technique and terminology and had a few attempts, you'll have a high assurance of success.
2. **Complicated problems** like building a rocket ship. These usually contain subsets of simple problems. Complicated problems sometimes require expertise and are not merely an assembly of simple components. However, rocket ships are similar in critical ways, so there is a high certainty of a good outcome.
3. **Complex problems** like managing people. Humans are non-linear. Every human is unique, so while managing one team member provides experience, it does not assure success with the next. Complex systems like human beings carry with them large elements of ambiguity and uncertainty.

People at work are complex. We try to aggregate them into nice little boxes with the likes of happiness surveys, performance management systems and myriad other processes. These systems have their place, but we must accept that no matter how much we corral teams and team members into systems and processes, we'll be forever surprised by their choices, reactions, and ability to make terrible or remarkable decisions.

I was brought up to treat others the way I'd like to be treated, but in business, we turn that on its head. You treat others the way *they'd* like to be treated. It's hugely empathic but requires emotional intelligence. Although some people display their emotions more than others, it doesn't mean that those who seem emotionless don't have emotions. Those I admire have a beautiful balance of IQ and EQ. They wear life loosely, without too much ego or the need to people please, pretend, or perfect. They're not afraid to show vulnerability, humour, joy, discomfort, or self-deprecation. They can operate well in ambiguity and uncertainty because of this balance. It's no surprise that therapists will point to black-and-white thinking as a symptom of a possible mental disturbance. Another classic symptom that therapists will consider is control. Trying to control others in an attempt to control yourself is clearly not healthy. Whether that means being overly nice or overly callous, the outcome is the same: an inauthentic relationship, built on sand.

Some believe that just talking about general anxieties in the workplace is inappropriate. 'Leave your emotions at the door' is a well-known tip from some old-fashioned managers. The only people who would seem to experience anxiety are those on the sick. Of course, this is ludicrous. We all feel what we feel, and how we react to emotions depends on many things. One of the most powerful counters to navigating unhelpful emotions is the EQ ability of an individual. Emotional intelligence significantly helps to manage emotions. It doesn't seek to numb, ignore, or pretend emotions are not there. EQ has the capacity to be aware, acknowledge, and accept any emotional state. EQ can refocus without pretending or people pleasing. This is authenticity at its best.

You don't have to be a brain surgeon to deduce that those who are defensive and moody and have poor relationships with their colleagues may need help in the EQ department. They may have vast cognitive abilities, but without some emotional competence, their capability to connect and engage with others will be limited, and their communication skills will be lacking. The result is that collaboration suffers, and so does productivity.

> Resumes don't perform, people do.
> So, hire people, not resumes!

Let me give you an example. When you employ someone, the first thresholds to pass are their basic competencies. Have they got the appropriate qualifications for the job and the experience gained from other employers that fits in with the skill set required? Once you've whittled down the applications to a shortlist, you invite them in for an interview. During an interview, you check an individual out to see if they understand the technical and intellectual competencies required for the job, but these questions have a discrete duality of purpose. As we ask these questions, we're also finding out whether we *like* the person. How are their interpersonal skills? Are they confident? If they stare at you, flirt, fart, or fidget, you judge them. And the barometer you use is EQ. Think about it in the context of sales. If the buyer doesn't like you, you're screwed.

Buyer's scenario	They like you	They don't like you
They really want it	Sold!	They'll buy it somewhere else
Not sure but marginally in favour	Very likely	Unlikely
Not sure but marginally against	Likely	Very unlikely
They don't want it	In your network, stay in touch	No chance. It's over

In interviews, we look at roundedness of character, interpersonal skills, empathy, tact, and consideration. Are we dealing with someone who's calm and confident, with integrity? Those with poor emotional intelligence cannot discern emotions well. They may dismiss them altogether. Have you ever been on an interview panel and a 'boss' has totally disregarded some emotional red flags because the candidate went to some posh university or has outstanding sales wins? Believe me, it happens all too often. To me, it's dangerous to ignore the stream of emotions that flow along with our stream of thoughts. We experience enormous amounts of emotions throughout our working day; pretending they don't exist is madness. Emotional intelligence manages this flow, and underneath the surface, we all seek the ability to manage emotions. Just check out what people google. I searched 'How not to be a ...' and got this:

- Awkward
- Annoying
- Anxious
- Angry
- A pushover
- A narcissist

Remember what I said at the start of the book: We don't see the world as it is; we see it as we are. And as you can see, many people want to change that.

The workplace is a professional environment, but it is inhabited by humans who are not robots. If you want to effectively communicate with your team, you'll most definitely need to top up your EQ skills.

Being in the team rather than above it means that you're going to have to learn how to manage relationships as well as how you respond to others. You became a manager because you have a specific knowledge of a workflow and have those necessary skills and expertise.

IQ tends to be task-oriented reasoning and objective logic, compared with EQ, which is based around people-oriented relationships, self-awareness, and managing emotions. We need both to be successful at managing others, but the scales are still weighed down in favour of IQ despite the overwhelming evidence. A study of UC Berkeley PhDs lasting over forty years found that EQ was four times more powerful than IQ in predicting who achieved success in their field. Therefore, IQ is no predictor of professional success (Trotta, 2018).

Managers have drifted into exclusive IQ waters because getting tasks done, achieving results and making a ton of cash is what business is all about, right? Except for one thing: we're dealing with human beings. People need human contact and connection.

Consider this. In the UK the absolute worst punishment we can give someone is solitary confinement. As a society we agree that solitary confinement is the harshest form of punishment we can bestow. Yet we are condemning ourselves to self-imposed solitary confinement every day. We dismiss connection as some 'weird, soft' thing and applaud the businesspeople who are great at imprisoning themselves and others into a regime that makes a USA supermax prison facility seem like a holiday camp! It's all fear, my friends. The guy in the sharp suit with an angry face doesn't intimate me, he saddens me. The woman with a hardened pout and heels so high she requires oxygen, saddens me. Don't get me wrong—sharp suits and heels are fantastic, but remember, we're not at war, and those who are stomping around the office infecting the populous with apathy are not impressive; they're destructive!

To me, EQ at work is best examined by the amount of time a manager spends with their team members. Great managers are interested in their team members, are rarely too busy for a 121, and genuinely want to connect with their people.

'High-IQ, low-EQ' managers avoid interaction. There is a plethora of reasons why they choose not to engage with others. Some are understandable, like being super busy, but are these really legitimate explanations or just avoidance excuses. Remember that solitude is a great place to visit but a terrible place to stay.

Many of us have been wounded by relationships in the past and therefore tread carefully. Carl Jung, the eminent psychologist, tells us that we are wounded by relationships but also healed by relationships.

The notion that some professionals are heartless is false (unless they're one of the dark triad—narcissists, machiavellians, and sociopaths). Most people are actually good-hearted folks. Someone's dad, mum, sister, cousin. They've loved and lost. They, we, you, do feel stuff like being trusted, supported, and valued. Managers/leaders need to become highly attuned to this.

According to Norwich University, things are getting worse as EQ scores among young people have fallen and average IQ scores have jumped (Norwich University, n.d.). However, remember what Brené Brown said: 'Empathy is a choice, a vulnerable choice' (The RSA, 2013). So, managers and team members need to lean into empathy and stop being so flippin' apathetic! That starts with understanding yourself a lot better.

This is nothing new. In fact, Socrates said, 'The unexamined life is not worth living.' Many others before and after him have simply said, 'Know thyself.' This is a no-brainer. How else are you expected to understand your strengths and weaknesses; how you cope with stress, manage conflict, and handle feedback? The list goes on. Discovering how you tick and therefore how you relate to those around you is vital to your success at work, especially as a manager. These are often known as 'soft' skills, but believe me, there's nothing soft about emotions. They can be intense and overpowering.

Feelings are like waves. You cannot stop them from coming, but you can decide which ones to surf. Surfing, like most pastimes, takes practice; but the first step is to understand the ocean and the basic techniques of surfing. I know nothing about surfing, but I have enough respect for the sea not to just grab a board and think I can master a ten-foot wave in five minutes or five weeks!

I firmly believe that having some intel on your emotions and then putting in counter measures is critical to your success. Back to the surfing analogy. It's a good idea to stop blaming the wave for being the reason you fell off the board. Frankly, you're not skilled enough. Here is a classic emotional wave. Look at the consequence. Basically, when you are at your angriest, you are also at your most stupid (KNILT, n.d.).

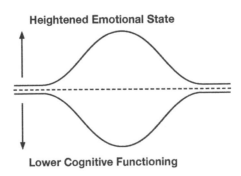

This also counts for any significant wave of emotion, from sadness to self-importance. How you gather, process, and express information will all be impeded significantly without EQ. Self-awareness helps you ride the emotional wave, which therefore diminishes any pronounced drop in your cognitive ability.

Let me give one example. Like the common cold, emotions are contagious. Caroline Bartel at New York University and Richard Saavedra at the University of Michigan studied seventy work groups across a variety of industries and found that people who worked together ended up sharing moods, good and bad (Bregman, 2018). Their moods converged. This is particularly important to understand for people in positions of authority because leaders, more than anyone, set and spread the mood. If you've ever worked in an office, you know this from experience. If the 'boss' is in a bad mood, conflicts increase. If they're in a good mood, people lighten up.

Look at it this way: if you catch a cold from someone, does that mean you can go around sneezing on everyone else? You might be able to blame your mood on someone else, but you're still responsible for what you pass on to others. This is a problem for businesses because mood affects performance. According to research done by Sigal Barsade at Yale University, positive moods improved cooperation, decreased conflict, and increased performance (Barsade, 2014).

There is plenty of evidence about how EQ can have a positive impact at work. In one study, one of the researchers concluded, 'A key takeaway is that soft values drive hard results' (AMA, 2019).

EQ is the ability to manage one's emotions and be aware of others' emotions. Start to discover your landmines. Who and what are the people, places, things, and situations that cause you to detonate the empathy and languish in apathy? It's worth reflecting.

Self-Awareness and Managing Your Emotions

Check out the *Johari window* (Wikipedia, n.d.). It's a great way to illustrate and improve self-awareness. It was invented by two American psychologists—one called Joseph, the other called Harrington, hence its name. There are four quadrants in the window, and it asserts that the more open we are, the more people will trust us. Go watch a YouTube video on this and then return to the book.

To reduce your 'blind spot', encourage more feedback, and to reduce the hidden area, make sure there's enough psychological safety in the workplace for people to feel OK when disclosing information that they may have felt difficult to normally share in a business environment.

There are tons of stuff online about the methodology. I use the *Johari window* often in coaching as a way to locate areas for improvement.

Take a personality test.

I am an MBTI practitioner. The MBTI is a personality test that helps identify your innate preferences (The Myers-Briggs Company, n.d.). There are tons of tests, but I have had the honour of seeing many, many eureka moments thanks to the MBTI.

These include the following:

- A managing director who loved the detail but everyone else on the leadership team preferred big picture. The MD's presentations were loathed by her team. The MBTI unlocked the 'why' and the 'how'. She now doesn't get too forensic, and relationships have transformed.
- A developer who thought he was stupid for not being able to answer questions 'off the cuff'. When he realised his need to think things through, he developed strategies to give him time to process questions, which seriously lowered his stress.
- A team that was fractured because of working practices only to see the differences in how one half of the team operate their lives compared to the other. This unlocked tensions, and now they love to collaborate.

Personality tests are part of my program. If you're going to train as a manager with me, I require that you take one as it will help you to understand yourself and understand others.

I quoted Dan Goleman earlier in this book. He's the godfather of emotional intelligence and wrote a book of the same name (Goleman, Emotional Intelligence, 2007). It's now widely accepted that EQ is separated into four areas to be examined: self-awareness and self-management. Social awareness and relationship management.

I've already suggested that you gather some intel on yourself (self-awareness) and get your colleagues to share their thoughts (social awareness). From that information, you'll be able to recognise some of the areas and learn techniques to regulate some unwanted behaviours.

As you've read, understanding your landmines will help you avoid any unwanted detonation. Whether that is your propensity to anger and the ability to manage it or your unfortunate habit of cutting others off mid-sentence. Maybe you're hopeless at small talk and find it difficult to genuinely connect with others. All these are opportunities to grow and the building blocks of empathy for yourself and others.

Low-EQ behaviours from colleagues and managers, such as angry outbursts and moodiness, lead to stress and burnout as well as anxious work environments. A study by Pearson and Porath (Porath & Pearson, 2013) of thousands of managers and employees concluded the following:

- Two-thirds of employees said their performance declined when working with others who had low EQ.
- Four out of five employees lost work time worrying about an unpleasant incident.
- 63 per cent wasted time avoiding the low-EQ offender.
- More than 75 per cent of respondents said that their commitment to their employer had waned.
- 12 per cent resigned due to the low-EQ behaviour.

We need to recognise and regulate emotions. I'm not in the business of getting you to morph into Mother Teresa. Simply become aware of yourself and others around you. This will be enough to recognise where you can regulate emotions that are unhelpful.

Over the next week, I want you to be mindful of your emotions. Keep a journal and write about the emotions you experience.

Answer these five questions about your feelings:

1. Can you identify and label your feelings correctly?
2. Are you able to assess the intensity of the feeling? Use a scale like 1–10.
3. How did you express the feeling?
4. How did you manage the feeling?
5. Did you have to control any impulses?

By shining a light on your emotions, you will become more self and socially aware and therefore be able to regulate your emotions much better.

Relationship Management Using the Drama Triangle

This triangle (Karpman, 2014) (The Karpman Drama Triangle, n.d.) has nothing to do with me but it's great. It's a nifty methodology that will really help you to steer away from drama and move into a meaningful dialogue with team members. It's been around for half a century, invented by a chap called Stephen Karpman, and cleverly maps out the three states we can find ourselves in when we're in some kind of conflict.

Here's how it looks:

The Drama Triangle

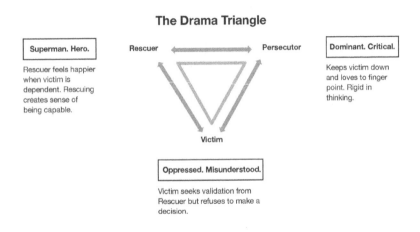

Superman. Hero.		Dominant. Critical.
Rescuer feels happier when victim is dependent. Rescuing creates sense of being capable.		Keeps victim down and loves to finger point. Rigid in thinking.

Rescuer ⟵⟶ Persecutor

Victim

Oppressed. Misunderstood.

Victim seeks validation from Rescuer but refuses to make a decision.

The three roles are:

- **Persecutor:** The villain
- **Victim:** Poor me, no one understands
- **Rescuer:** Superman or Wonder Woman (take your pick)

You can drop into the Triangle playing one role, but in just one conversation find yourself playing every role! Let me give you an example. Employee Adam (the victim) comes to you complaining that his co-worker Jane (the persecutor) is making his life really difficult and being dismissive towards him since they fell out about something two days ago. Adam and Jane have been friendly co-workers for years and have occasional spats, but Adam says it's starting to affect his work. You, the manager (the rescuer), bring them both into the office for a chat to clear the air. The scene is set, we all have our roles, and now the drama can truly begin.

You tell Jane to stop her dismissive behaviour. Suddenly, Jane breaks down and Adam goes over and comforts her. Suddenly, you are the persecutor, Jane is the victim and Adam is the rescuer! After a moment, Adam has a go at you for being harsh with her, but Jane pipes up and asks everyone to calm down. Now you're the victim, Adam is the persecutor, and Jane is the rescuer!

I love this model. I'm sure you can remember situations when you've found yourself trying to be helpful but actually not helping at all.

The solution is to become mindful of the drama triangle when in tricky conversations, making sure you don't fall into the trap of playing the role of persecutor, victim, or rescuer.

Instead, attempt to leverage these traits:

The Drama Triangle - The Solution

Coach	Rescuer		Persecutor	Challenger
• More Yoda, less Superman • Encourage options • Have boundaries				• Set clear expectations • Actively listen • Set boundaries

Victim

Creator
• State what you want
• Take action
• Focus on your strengths
• An attitude of gratitude

Personally, I can easily fall into the rescuer role, which actually disempowers the victim and keeps them where they are. What does the victim learn if I whoosh in like Superman every time they come up against conflict? It's the 'give the man a fish or teach him how to fish' analogy. So, when I feel I'm rescuing, I mindfully shift into coaching. Instead of fixing the problem, I help them work it out for themselves by listening and questioning.

Victims often have a 'yes, but ...' attitude, so help them work out what they really want and then take action towards that goal. Persecutors need to stop talking and start listening. You may well have not clearly articulated what you wanted. When it's time, challenge, but be careful not to persecute! Notice though the importance of setting boundaries. Compassion has boundaries. I will buy a homeless person a sandwich, but I don't offer them to stay at my place. In the same way here, be clear about what you can do and what they are responsible for.

So next time you find yourself in a drama, move into the solution roles, and you'll be able to really help people. In fact, share this model to help resolve the conflict. There is tons of stuff about the drama triangle online (The Karpman Drama Triangle, n.d.), but this should be enough info to use it effectively.

The way we conduct ourselves at work does have certain constraints. For example, the way we behave with colleagues or our ability to focus is driven by the conditions of our employment, but there is a line. Being professional does not mean P'ing your power away by:

> Almost all absurdity of conduct arises from the imitation of those whom we cannot resemble.
>
> **—Samuel Johnson**

Proving: Showing that you're better than others or that you have more than others. Problem is, someone will have a bigger car, have a better house, be more experienced, and know more of the right people. Proving is a thankless and ultimately frustratingly bad game. From bitter experience, trust me, it will never be enough.

Plotting: Manipulating your way through life, avoiding situations that are too tricky, or blaming others for mistakes that you should be holding your hands up to.

Panicking: Catastrophising situations. Letting emotions shoot off randomly and allowing phobias to take hold. Persecuting yourself daily.

Pandering: Becoming submissive for the sole purpose of getting what you want. You end up losing yourself in other people's wants.

Predicting: Mind-reading others in the hope that you'll work out what they want and then give it to them. Problem is, you can't mind-read.

Performing: Deflecting—becoming the clown or the ultimate cynic.

Perfecting: Incredibly damaging but used all the time in modern parlance. Perfection is a myth; it does not exist, and to strive for it means constant disappointment. Try aiming for excellence.

People Pleasing: Trying to keep everyone else happy while ignoring your own needs. Empathy is important, but not at the cost of your well-being.

Procrastinating: Putting off dreams or not acting on opportunities because of fear. Pigeonholing yourself. There is also a weird inertia place. You know what you need to do, but energy is sapped and willpower depleted.

Pretending: Acting like everything is fine when inside you're holding back a tsunami of stuff. Putting a brave face on only works some of the time. Lots of people see right through it, so stop kidding yourself.

> Be who you are today because when tomorrow comes, you'll have to try to remember who you pretended to be yesterday.
>
> **—Author Unknown**

Tools: Emotional Intelligence

1. Check out the work of Dan Goleman and his Emotional Intelligence Model.
2. Take a personality test and use the Johari window to gain more insights.
3. Use the Drama Triangle as a way of increasing emotional intelligence.

Contextualises Communication

As a manager, it's vital to communicate with confidence, handle conflict, and navigate tricky conversations. This is where most of the challenges for managers are, from dealing with more senior stakeholders (managing up) to having meaningful performance conversations with team members. Patrick Lencioni, in his book *The Five Dysfunctions of a Team* (Lencioni, 2002), calls this out as 'fear of conflict' and names the result as 'artificial harmony'. To be really honest, most managers lack skill in this area. As a manager, it's vital to have the ability to communicate with confidence, not shy away from conflict, and navigate tricky conversations with purpose.

> The biggest problem with communication is the illusion that it has taken place.
>
> **—George Bernard Shaw**

Firstly, I want you to understand the importance of being super clear in any communication. Any nuance may be misinterpreted and misunderstood.

That's why the saying in presentation skills training still holds true to this day: 'Tell them, tell them what you just told them, then tell them again.' Misunderstandings, misinterpretations, confusion, and exaggeration can all lead to confusion and error, which then make us conclude there must be incompetence, clumsiness, and inefficiency. Here, trust is seriously threatened. This is all because the message *you* gave was misinterpreted. How many times have you heard, 'Oh, sorry, I thought you meant ...'?

It's your responsibility to make sure the message has landed correctly. Please confirm they have really understood you. Ask them to play back your needs, just to be sure they're on the right track. Check out 'Sets Clear Expectations' for more top tips.

Effective Feedback

Be careful of your intent. Managing conflict comes from a place of empathy, not ego! Be consistent and praise the good stuff; don't just work on the 'bad' stuff. Basically, if you give team members attention only when things need improvement, they will associate you with negative connotations, and it will be difficult for them to really listen as they wrestle with a threat response.

Let me be absolutely clear about feedback: it is neither positive nor negative. As soon as you 'charge' the feedback with this sort of descriptive energy, you and the recipient are in danger of avoiding 'negative' feedback. Feedback is either constructive or it's not. Let's cut to the chase with some key differences between constructive feedback and criticism:

Constructive	Criticism
Observation-based evidence	Interpretations and judgements
Problem focused	Person focused
Information specific	Opinions
Empathic	Ego based
Informal	Formal

Notice a few things here. First of all, if there is no clear example (evidence), then it is not feedback. It is just an opinion, and there is no place in feedback for your or anybody else's opinion. Maybe you weren't there, but you need clear, observation-based evidence on any issue for it to be warranted as constructive feedback. Feedback is best received as close to the event as possible, as long as emotions are cool. Feedback will not be given or received well in high emotional states. On these occasions I recommend you allow some 'time out' for heads to cool before feedback is initiated.

> Feedback is a free education to excellence.
>
> Seek it with sincerity and receive it with grace.
>
> **—Ann Marie Houghtailing**

The next point is to keep your feedback problem focused and not person focused. Don't talk about them; talk about their behaviour. It helps make them less defensive. For example: 'This anger has to stop' rather than 'You need to stop being so angry.' This is not HR BS—there is a real danger that your feedback won't be heard if you target the person and not the problem. And the reason is that their threat response has been evoked by criticising and not being constructive. You can be candid; just make sure you're not pointing the finger at the person but rather at the problem. This takes a little practice to master.

Another reason feedback is not taken seriously that you give too much of it once you've got into the flow. Have you ever been in a relationship where you had a little argument that turned out to be a massive showdown with instances from years ago being brought up? It's exactly the same when poor team leaders fail to give regular feedback. A tipping point arises and an unskilled manager flips. A torrent of old resentment floods the feedback, and the outcome is a more disengaged member of staff. So, keep your feedback short and focused on one topic at a time.

Watch out for something else I've come across, which my friend Brendan, an experienced manager, explains beautifully. Beware of folks who say, 'Just tell me how it is, no BS. Just get to the point.' My experience has shown that these people are particularly sensitive. Now I agree, get to the point quickly, but be careful to be as empathic as you would be with anyone else. As Brendan said, 'Everybody says they want you to be direct with them, as long as you're not direct with them!'

Here's an awesome trick I use. Be a puller and not a pusher. When you're talking to anyone, and especially in feedback, use pulling tactics and not pushing ones.

Pushing	Pulling
Demanding	Active listening
Stating positions	Questioning
Past tense	Future tense
Yes, but ...	Yes, and ...

I love this in class because it works every time. I ask someone to put their hand out in front of them, as if they're asking me to stop. I then push their hand back and, guess what, they push back every time. *Every time.* This is human behaviour. When someone pushes you, you push back. Therefore, we need to find better tactics than just 'pushing' people. Pulling behaviours are the answer, not because they're less challenging but rather because the team member really feels heard and is therefore way more likely to consider and implement an agreed solution. Once again that gorgeous little phrase punches through: 'When others feel heard by you, they're more likely to listen to you.'

So, when giving feedback that you find to be a little difficult, use my tool called the '4X Model': explain, examples, explore, expedite.

The 4X Feedback Model

Explain
In a sentence, explain the reason for the feedback

Examples
Have clear examples of the behaviour

Expedite
Agree on a way to move forward

Explore
Ask open questions and actively listen to their explanation

Explain: Very briefly explain the reason for the feedback. Be specific.

> *We agreed that this project was to be signed off yesterday, but it's still not finished.*

Examples: Provide a clear example to objectively demonstrate the behaviour you're discussing. Be specific.

> *Emails regarding the deadline and the OKR with the date, or a note from last week's stand-up saying everything was good.*

Explore: Genuinely find out their side of the story. Actively listen; take notes. 'Can you help me understand what's going on?' Remember that most people listen with the intent to reply and not understand. Make sure you're not one of them. Stay open and make a genuine attempt to listen.

> *Employee says his wife's father has died, and he's been upset as well as dealing with his wife's grief.*

Expedite: Agree on a way to move forward. Only impose a plan in extraordinary circumstances. Compromise a little. Find a middle ground.

> *Be concerned for his and his wife's wellbeing. Is the deadline extendable? Or can someone else jump in? Maybe you can help out. These are the times when your team needs you. Show support and cut him some slack.*

The 4X Model really works. I've had awesome feedback about it, but it does take practice. My advice is to keep it as simple as possible, taking it step by step; and in steps one, two, and four, be as specific as possible. Being vague never punches through. Also, lousy managers just go from explain straight to expedite, 'You're late. Don't do it again,' as if that's going to work! Remember what I just said about pushing. So practise this model regularly for it to stick.

Managing Up

Beware: if your leader is apathetic, they're contagious!

Over the years, many of my clients have asked about the best way to manage their manager. I worry about what sort of behaviour they're trying to handle. On deeper enquiry, it comes as no surprise that leaders (your manager's manager) can often display arrogance and apathy. People are complex no matter what level of the business they're in, but some leaders thrive on power and control. A select few are sociopaths with little or no understanding of empathy. Others fall into the dark triad. I coached one leader who was thrilled when I suggested he had Machiavellian traits. So, if you're concerned about how to manage up effectively, please be as socially aware as you are self-aware. It might not be you who is the problem! You don't have to consistently tolerate rotten behaviour. We all have 'bad' days, but you deserve a workplace where you can thrive and not fight to survive. However, always lean into empathy first. You probably have little idea of the realities of your leader's life or the pressure which is being exerted on them.

With all that in mind, there are a few tricks that can help you achieve a better working relationship with your manager:

- If they ask for ABC, don't give them CDE. Give them what they asked for, not what you think they want. Once you have successfully given them ABC, that opens the doorway to suggest D and E.
- They don't like surprises. Forewarned is forearmed, so keep them informed of any changes in the landscape that you're responsible for.
- Problem and solution: clearly define the problem as you see it and give them options for a solution.
- They love data, so be evidence-based. Work out processes that provide data quickly. Pulling off regular reports with meaningful data will make them very happy.
- Only the top line: give more detail only when requested. Don't get into the weeds with leaders unless they ask for detail. Keep your conversations big picture so that you focus on the *vital few* and not the *trivial many*.
- Ask for their communication preferences. Do they prefer an email or a quick meeting to be scheduled rather than you

pouncing on them? Always contextualise communication to their preference.

Many have found these suggestions to be super helpful, but beware: if your leader is apathetic, their apathy can be highly contagious! Guard yourself against becoming apathetic. There's an old saying: 'If you keep going to the barbers, you'll end up getting your hair cut.' Be mindful of your boundaries and what you determine to be acceptable behaviour.

One area that it is important to understand as you rise up the ranks is the politics of an organisation. Not only will you be responsible for more people's productivity, but you'll also have to manage the politics of leadership. This can be frustrating for managers who just want to drive for results but find themselves having to play the diplomat. Sometimes you'll need to work out how to move forward when you're getting several different messages from the leadership team. That's why clear expectations, written down and signed off, are so important. I remember being told to do something by my manager, and his manager came up to me and was clearly confused about why I'd done that particular task above another one. Politics can be baffling to the uninitiated. Ignore it at your cost. Try not to get too involved, but certainly be aware of the game that's being played out.

The solution is to play the diplomat. Dwight Eisenhower said, 'A diplomat is a person who is paid to think before he says nothing.' Don't gossip; do remain objective and honour your values. Stay true to yourself. It will always guide you home in the mists of managing politics.

Presenting with Confidence

Being a competent communicator is critical in business, especially as a team leader. For me, the competency lies in the ability to connect with your audience and not talk at them. Slick doesn't impress me, especially if there's no humility. If you can transcend the nonsense of pretending and the fears that make you pander or panic, then the result can be mesmerising. In this section, I share my top tips on how to present with confidence. From presenting at a huge conference to sharing a short story at an all-hands, I'll share some top tips and techniques that I know work. My first career, before moving into coaching, was a TV and radio broadcaster. I had a good stint and won Presenter of the Year at the BBC. Since then, I have presented in many different corporate settings, so I know these suggestions work.

This section will help you when delivering in a meeting, a company get-together or a larger presentation. Let's start big, so settle in and let me tell you a story about a speaking engagement I had at a conference.

I'm in a towering posh five-star hotel overlooking the Danube. It's a chilly morning in Budapest. Commuters are briskly walking to work with their freezing breath bellowing on the exhale like an overworked steam locomotive. The imposing state buildings across the river are wrapped in mist. This scene could easily be a spooky opening for any dodgy vampire movie. However, I'm not here to fang a local (that sounds so wrong); I'm here to make a speech at a big conference.

Now, I want you to really imagine you are about to take my place. As you read on, become conscious of how you'd feel at the prospect of getting on the stage and addressing the audience.

The event is in a massive ballroom about the size of two football pitches. It's huge, with amazing twinkly chandeliers hanging over the thirty circular tables. There's an enormous set with a stage, two mega-screens, and cameras, lights, the works. Waiters are everywhere servicing the 250 suited professionals who are pouring in after a big night out on the company, all 250 of them to listen to me. It's 9 a.m., and I'm first on. They're hung-over and no doubt a little grumpy. Some of them are pale with a little grimace (maybe they *are* vampires!). They're all feverishly networking. The gabble of the

crowd gets louder and louder until the MC shouts, 'Good morning!'
I'm on.

Pause your powers of imagination.

If that sort of scenario is something that fills you with dread,
but you need to conquer your fears - never fear - Davies is here! If
you get the jitters, can't seem to make an impact, turn into a robot,
can't get your words out, feel judged, and can't connect with your
audience, then I am your knight in shining armour on my trusty
horse. Well, actually, forget the horse. The prospect of getting on
a horse fills me with dread! Lesson one: we all have fears. I guess
the difference is I don't want to be a jockey or need to ride a horse
in my day-to-day work. But many of us have to make presentations
in our business life. It's that necessity I wish to address so you can
make a presentation without freezing, forgetting, or just falling flat.
But it's more than that. You want your presentation to be successful.
For me, success is down to whether you can connect with your
audience. The ultimate way to do that is to be yourself on stage. If
you can tap into your authenticity, the real you, I promise that your
presentations will take on a new power that will really break through
to the assembled crowd.

It all boils down to the ability to communicate with confidence.
It's all literally show business, so get your teeth stuck into this section
of the book. No more vampire puns—I promise.

Inform and Motivate

I love these two beauties. Informing is IQ: understanding
the price, product, specification, SAP, and people requirements.
Motivation is EQ and more heart led, founded on principles like
trust, belief, and meaningful relationships. You need both in a
presentation. The mistake is that we either inform or motivate.
The solution is to have a healthy mixture of both characteristics.
Updating the leadership with relevant information is crucial, but

you must also compel them (motivation). Just informing them will lack energy and purpose. I think it's lazy to start your presentation by apologising for the dullness of the content. You need to find a way to link the data with destiny. It's a bit like features and benefits in sales. If the data is seriously dull (features), what are the benefits of looking at it (benefits)?

For example, think of a car:

Features	Benefits
0–60 mph in five seconds	Able to get home faster to tuck the kids in.
Heated seats	For someone with chronic lower back pain, they can seriously ease any discomfort.
Optimised sound placement	Helps those who are hearing impaired, and in times when a call is too loud in the front and too quiet in the back.

Do the same with your data. Talk about features only if you can articulate the benefits.

Interested versus Interesting

Presentations need to be conversations. We put so much pressure on ourselves to shine in the spotlight, but the secret is to put the audience in the spotlight, not you! Presentations need to be conversations. No matter how big the audience, become fascinated, listen, and stay curious about the person or people you're talking with. Do not interrogate, but do be intrigued about their views. Listen carefully and respond with more questions. Everyone has a fascinating story to tell. I don't say that lightly. As a former broadcaster, I've presented more than three thousand radio talk shows, and one thing I didn't do was talk blandly to a caller about the weather. I got my researchers to dig a little, and when the caller came on air, we'd get into some great tales. For example, one listener (who I'll call John) recalled how he turned down The Beatles from performing at his club because they wanted £400 for the gig and he offered them only £150.

People's lives, all of them, are extraordinary, and if you have the capacity to become curious and stay captivated, they will open up. Now, it can take some gentle persuasion. You may well get one-word answers to start with, but as you continually cajole, you'll tickle out these tales and receive other added benefits like humour, honesty, and wholeheartedness.

Here's a secret that's worth bearing in mind when you're force-feeding your views down the throats of clients or colleagues: basically, they don't care how great you are until they understand that you know how great they are!

Hence, your presentation needs to be super interactive. Involve them at every turn, and please question why somebody wants your presentation to be longer than fifteen minutes. Think TED Talks. Aren't they long enough? Hollywood blockbusters can cost around $250,000 a minute to produce. This is what you're up against. So, if you're on for an hour, split your presentation into fifteen-minute chunks and get your audience involved. Your secret weapon is the ability to interact. Most of the time, you're in front of professionals who know what you're talking about. Treat them as such. Do not lecture them. Rather, use their expertise.

I often use the analogy of the conductor and the orchestra. Shaky presenters try to be both and fail miserably. Treat a presentation like you're the conductor and the audience is the orchestra. I promise you'll know when you're making 'great music' because there'll be energy coming back off the audience.

Nine ways to interact:

1. Do an icebreaker exercise.
2. Get them to do stuff in small groups. Some little exercise that demonstrates a point you're making.
3. Ask them questions.
4. Plant some testimonials for people to read out.
5. Interview someone you've set up in the audience.
6. Take a poll.
7. Ask them what they're looking to get out of your presentation.
8. Use props and involve audience members.
9. Ask them what their takeaways from the presentation are.

The Three R's

The prospect of presenting to colleagues or clients will mean you are literally being called to account—called to account for your people, the processes, your product, and the price. You can't pass the buck. You're in the spotlight with no hiding place. However, unless you've just joined your company and you're unfamiliar with its practices, the truth is you know the answer to most of the questions you could be asked, and if you don't, there are three simple steps which will reassure you that all is in order. These steps are called the 'Three Rs'.

Research

Don't just show up and throw up! What does the audience need? Always their needs, never your wants! Do your homework and find out. Talk to those who are attending and ask them. Get them to be explicit. What do they want to get from you? Once you get that information, you refer to it during your presentation. 'Michelle, I know you are particularly interested in the financials, so here is the information ...'

Remember that quote from *Getting to Yes*: 'When others feel heard by you, they're more likely to listen to you.' So do your research and do it proudly.

Your presentation should clearly understand the audience's dilemma and then solve it. If you're pitching, this is critical. If you're presenting findings, what and how you present will depend on who is in the audience. The expectations of a creative crowd will be very different from those of accountants. Always encourage them to interact. I prefer to get the main body of my presentation out before opening up to the floor as some of their answers will most probably be in my content. Then I allow them to dig deeper by asking questions.

> Judge a person by their questions, rather than their answers.
>
> **—Voltaire**

I remember sitting in a large international conference surrounded by senior managers. They were listening to a high-end market research company share findings from some expensive research they'd been commissioned to do regarding sales. The number-one recommendation was 'Be reactive to the customer's needs.'

I know it's obvious, but this is a recurring theme in business — people pushing their product or service to prospective clients who want something else. You can often provide that 'something', but you have to find out what it is before you pitch or present.

It's not all about you! It's about the audience's needs rather than your wants. Therefore, you need to be asking questions, understanding your audience and accepting that one size does not fit all. If you haven't done your homework about the audience you're presenting to, you're wasting your time.

> Never try to teach a pig to sing. It wastes your time and just annoys the pig.
>
> **—George Bernard Shaw**

Review

Once you've gathered all the information, ask a trusted colleague to look through it. You need a second opinion. This will reassure you that you have the correct data. This is not about passing the buck; this is best practice in action. Offices can suffer from silo syndrome. Keeping to yourself and not asking for help just in case they think you're stupid—an example of psychological safety impeding performance. However, we need each other. So get out there and talk to your colleagues. Not only will the quality of your work improve, but so will your confidence about the presentation and its contents.

Rehearse

The magic behind a great presentation is practice. Don't bother with a pitch if you're going in half ready. It baffles me that we spend so much time on moving a graphic a little bit more to the left or right but don't find the time to really rehearse the content. It's a no-brainer: the more you rehearse, the better you will be. It is nonsense that the magic will somehow disappear if you rehearse too much. You can always improve. Sportspeople know this too well.

> If I don't practice the way I should, then I won't play the way that I know I can.
>
> — Ivan Lendl, successful tennis player in the late 80s

However, people often don't think that rehearsing is necessary for meetings or networking. They're wrong! How do you introduce yourself in a networking scenario? Go to a mirror, do it, and tell me if you'd want to hang out with that person. Don't kid yourself that those who sparkle in such circumstances haven't been coached for networking and meetings. I know because I've coached a few myself! So practise your introductions and rehearse your 'funny' stories. The same with meetings. Go through the agenda out loud with a colleague. The more you rehearse, the better you'll be (obviously). So, why aren't you doing it more?

Oh, by the way, practice *never* makes perfect. Perfect doesn't exist. Practice makes you better, for sure, but perfection is a pipe dream. Be excellent and do your best, but striving for an insane goal is stressful and, frankly, unattainable.

> My secret is practice.
>
> **—David Beckham**

Presenting Mini Presentations

Here's a nifty little tool that can keep you on track when presenting an idea to your team:

What?	So what?	Now what?
Clearly define the subject matter. Don't bury the headline. If you can't describe it concisely, you don't know the subject well enough.	Why now? Compared with everything else we're doing, why should this take precedence? Be careful to show the benefits and not just the features.	If we were to go ahead, what would the implications be? How much would it cost, who would be involved, and how long would it take? *SMART* goals.

Presenting Larger Presentations Using AIDA

I've used a tool that advertisers and marketers have successfully used for a century to engage their audiences. It works beautifully for presentations and pitches. It also translates to meetings and spicing up your networking stories.

It's called the 'AIDA' methodology (Wikipedia, n.d.), and it's really simple. There are four steps:

1. **A**ttention
2. **I**nterest
3. **D**esire
4. **A**ction

It will help you ignite your narrative and is absolutely awesome if you want your story to soar.

Attention: Grab them straight away. How are you going to really get the attention of your audience? Never bury a great story. Don't build up to a big announcement—put it at the top of your presentation. Many great presenters immediately interact with their audience, so maybe ask a question. It'll wake up your audience as they have to pay attention because you may ask them another question.

- Ask them a question
- Guess a stunning statistic
- Work out the missing piece of a headline

My favourite story about finding a great headline is a tale I cannot verify, but hey, never let the truth get in the way of a good story, right? I'm told it's true and is legendary. Two movie wannabes had the chance to pitch their film to a top Hollywood movie mogul. They were understandably nervous. This could be their big break, and they recognised that they wouldn't get this chance again anytime soon, so they were determined not to screw things up. They excitedly talked for hours about this meeting. They had written the script, so they knew the storyline inside and out, but when the time came to pitch, nerves got the better of them, and they waffled, got mixed up, and basically made the narrative sound so complicated that the movie mogul was getting a headache. However, he gave them a second chance by asking them to step out of his office, go and get a coffee, and try to simmer down what the film was about into a short sentence or, better still, three words. Off they went. They returned an hour later. The movie man leant forward in his big leather chair, cigar in mouth. 'Hit me with it, fellas,' he said.

With a glint in their eyes, they replied, '*Jaws* in space,' and the *Alien* saga was born.

Can you make a headline up about the presentation you're putting together? If you can't, I suggest it's too complicated and not focused enough. If you can't explain your presentation in a few words, do you honestly think other people are going to understand what it's about? If I'm feeling particularly cheeky with clients, I'll take them outside, give them a matchbox, and ask them to light a match and explain their presentation before the match burns their fingers. It certainly focuses the mind.

Interest: So what? Now you've got their attention, it's time to explain the attention grabber in more detail. This is where you can demonstrate your expertise on the given subject. Be careful not to set yourself apart from your audience—be with them. No one likes a smartass, so show some vulnerability through empathy. We learn by our mistakes, so display your humanity. Remember that vulnerability is not weakness—it's a sure way to connect with others.

You must demonstrate your understanding of the audience's needs. What I mean is that you may well be setting the agenda with your presentation, but if you don't understand the audience's agenda, then you'll fail. For example, I was working on a conference and a fellow speaker came to do an inspiring talk. He was great, but one member of staff said that it bore little relevance to their business. Yes, the themes the speaker spoke about could be translated to most areas of corporate life, but he failed to explicitly show that relevance. So talk about them (the audience), and make sure what you're talking about clearly and unequivocally makes sense for their roles and responsibilities.

- **Real:** Don't tell them; show them through real examples.
- **Relevant:** A credible and clear understanding of their needs.
- **Responsive:** Interact. Rhetorical questions or a quick poll with hands.

Desire: Yes, please! You've got their attention and shown you understand their needs, so it's time to create an appetite. It's a bit like conjuring up that smell of food that makes you want to eat something. The 'interest' shows them you understand the recipe and the ingredients as well as the cooking instructions, etc.

This is where you show them the cake, just out of the oven!

- Why you, why now?
- FAB: features and benefits.
- Demonstrate success with examples of trust and relationships.

Action: Make them do something. Keeping with the 'desire' cake analogy, offer them a slice.

- Desire triggers action—so don't skip the desire step.
- Add value with websites, handouts, Q&As, and networking after the presentation.
- Don't be afraid to instigate action. Move through natural inertia and caution.

That last point is so important. As I was once told, 'Don't be backwards in coming forwards.' You don't have to be pushy, but you can offer them the opportunity to sign on the dotted line. As you can see, you're seeking some form of action. If you're in a small meeting, what are the action points and who's going to do them? At a larger presentation, encourage audience members to come and see you to get a free copy of a white paper you've put together.

There are tons of tips to help you take your presentation to the next level. Here's a quick list to consider:

1. Fail to prepare, prepare to fail—don't write it the night before.
2. Record yourself and watch yourself back (webcam on your laptop or a smartphone).
3. Create atmosphere (room temp., lighting).
4. Get to the point and keep it short. Why more than fifteen minutes?
5. The power of the parable—show them, don't tell them.
6. Evidence—use examples and share some fascinating facts.
7. Read out testimonials; let other people tell your story.
8. Remember, it's a dialogue, not a monologue.
9. Respect your audience—keep to your time.
10. Intention. If your intention is clear, your message will be clear.

Your Slides

Please keep your content uncluttered and simple. It's better to have an image or one word on a slide. Remember, your slides are not your aide-memoire. Slides are often cluttered for the presenter's benefit. It's OK to have notes in your hand. I am not a designer, so work with one.

Performing Your Presentation

You are showing off your business, so this is literally *show business*. Raise your game, and remember: to compel, you have to be compelling. Watch out that you're not 'erming' too much. It gives the audience the feeling that you're not confident about your subject. It's super easy to stop erming. Just become mindful of it. Slow down and pause instead of erming. Practise this by recording yourself and speaking on any topic for thirty seconds. Removing the erms really cleans up the message and increases your credibility. You do this simply by becoming more mindful of them. Have some fun with colleagues by asking them to give you random subjects to talk about, *but* you can't say 'erm' (no lists, either). Have a moderator check your erms. It's not as easy as you think.

Engage the room by making clear eye contact with as many people as you can. Finally, remember, you're probably the only person who knows what you're about to say. The audience doesn't. So take a chill pill if you mix something up or leave something out. They'll never know!

Finally, for this section, always centre yourself before you present. Practising mindfulness will seriously help you. Decide to enjoy rather than endure this moment. By shining, you will literally light up the room. Positive energy is contagious, so get your mindset in the right place, and you'll be surprised at how easy presentations are. Be the energy you want to create.

Tools: Contextualises Communication

1. Apply the 4X Feedback Model. Be a puller, not a pusher.
2. Learn and apply the techniques of managing up.
3. Apply all the preparation and performance tips, such as AIDA, to your presentations.

Coaches and Mentors

This is all about learning and development. Be obsessed with mastery. Learn every day and encourage your team to set personal development goals.

> Leadership and learning are indispensable to each other.
>
> **—John F. Kennedy**

You can get so caught up in delivering that you forget to develop. If team members don't feel they are developing in their careers, then they will leave and go somewhere that does help them to progress. In smaller companies, there is less room to get promoted but still plenty of opportunities to develop. That means a development plan that includes tons of learning. This should not be a passive experience for your team. They need to own their personal development; you just need to encourage and support it. Encourage them to watch TED Talks and then bring their learnings to the team. Are they building their own LinkedIn network and attending different events? Learning need not be spoon-fed; there are so many sources of learning. Take a holistic approach that combines many sources. If a team member is not doing these things, you may want to investigate further. Have they really reached the end of the rainbow of learning? Do they really know best? Continuous personal development (CPD) is a joint venture between you and your team member rather than something imposed from above, so make it a collaborative exercise.

Make sure that the learning you agree on suits the team member. I have seen people slowly drown in MBAs or sign up to boring online courses that could cure insomnia. The writer Brian Herbert said it beautifully: 'The capacity to learn is a gift, the ability to learn is a skill, the willingness to learn is a choice.'

Some people are more academic than others, so the style of learning needs to be considered. One solution that works for most is 'show me, don't tell me'. Content that is not contextualised is interesting but not meaningful, and it is therefore easily forgotten. Make sure any learnings have relevance to the individual and can be implemented. Herbert talks about learning being a skill. I agree. You need to learn how to learn. I recommend you try to learn something every week and chronicle it in your weekly reports. Finally, he succinctly says that the willingness to learn is a choice. It keeps a growth mindset to the foreground.

One top tip is to create a personal development plan (PDP) for every member of staff alongside their appraisal. The appraisal looks back, and the PDP looks forward. I suggest three goals. Make sure they're *SMART*! (More on SMART goals in the expertise domain).

Coaching

Most people agree that coaching is more directional, work related, and solution focused, whereas mentoring is more person focused. The latter is about listening, reflecting, and helping the mentee to reach their own decision. For example, mentoring can help with career development. Make sure you're offering both coaching and mentoring in your relationships. Your 121s should be mentoring activities rather than coaching opportunities. However, if the team member chooses not to learn or develop, then it's near impossible to make an impact. Hence the necessity to overtly encourage a learning culture. If team members don't want to learn, they're in the wrong tribe and need to find a company who wallow in fixed mindsets.

When I'm coaching, one of the tools I use the GROW model (MindTools, n.d.). It was devised by Graham Alexander, Alan Fine, and Sir John Whitmore. It's based on the theory that using questions rather than instructions in a coaching session will foster change more readily. The acronym GROW stands for goal, reality, options, and will. It's a simple framework for structuring a coaching session and has been adopted by many of the world's major organisations. Have a coaching session at the moment of need. This should be happening regularly. The GROW model is an awesome agenda setter and road map for these conversations.

- **Goal:** A target to be reached in the session must be decided. Make sure it's a *SMART* goal. This is often developed and decided on with a little help from the next stage, so don't worry if you're hopping between goal and reality.
- **Reality:** It is important that this session is grounded in reality. The person being coached should be able to assess their present situation and use the reality stage to hone the goal. Focus on concrete examples rather than perceptions.

Challenge their perspective but don't dominate. Get all the issues on the table before moving to the next stage.

- **Options:** This stage offers the opportunity for the person being coached to suggest possible courses of action. Allow them to come up with the options. Help, don't dominate. Another tip at this stage is not to get stuck into issue-option-issue-option. Make sure all the issues are on the table in the 'reality' stage. This stage is simply about brainstorming rather than trying to find a solution. Maybe use post-it-notes to gather a few different options.

- **Will:** The final part of the process involves the person being coached to make decisions. They need to decide which options to commit to. Future steps to be taken should be confirmed, and the coach should agree with the coachee how they will be supported through the ongoing development process.

Here are some questions to consider for each stage:

Goal:

- Where would you like to be in …?
- What outcome do you want from this process?
- What would be the best outcome from your perspective?
- What would you like to achieve?

Reality:

- What's happening for you?
- How are you feeling about what is happening?
- What other factors are relevant?
- What have you tried so far?

Options:

- What could you do to change the situation?
- What alternatives are there to that approach?
- What approaches have you used in similar situations?
- What would happen if you did nothing?

Will and way forward:

- Which option would you like to put into action?
- What would be your first step?
- What further support do you need?
- Who could support you?

It is important to be aware that at all times in this process the coachee is gently being nudged towards developing their own action plan rather than being ordered along a certain route.

Mentoring

I believe mentoring is nurturing activity, so these words, mentoring and nurturing are interchangeable. Whenever I point the finger at someone, I'm starkly aware I have three fingers pointing back at me! In this section I'll be looking at nurturing oneself and others. Before we get into mentoring, it's worthwhile examining *who* we're mentoring. I've already described a mentoring intervention (regular 121s), so I'm going to go deep now. Enough of the baby pool; let's get into the deep end! I want you to nurture the real rather than pander to the fake. Use this section as an opener to a deeper discussion about self-discovery and the reasons behind why we create false personas and end up mentoring the bogus instead of the beautiful.

It's Not the Crime. It's the Cover-Up

If you're not familiar with the famous saying 'It's not the crime. It's the cover-up', it came from the Watergate scandal in the USA back in the 1970s. Although some tried to dismiss it as a botched burglary, the attempt to acquire and cover up alleged dodgy campaign practices from the Democratic National headquarters eventually came back to haunt the highest man in office. As the story's full impact was felt by the American public, the press and Congress lifted the lid off a whole range of illegal and improper campaign activities. This resulted in President Richard Nixon being impeached and eventually resigning. 'It's not the crime. It's the cover-up' shows us that we've all done things we're not proud of. However, the persistent denial of what is real is the context in which I use this phrase.

We all have foibles, failings and fears which we want to be kept hidden; but if you hang out with someone for a relatively short space of time, they do shine through, and my point is *That's OK!* In fact, the very reason I hang out with people isn't that they're all pretending to be something they're not; it's because I love their individual preferences and characteristics. What they may have thought to be their weakness is, in fact, their strength. The clue is the word 'personal' in 'personality'! It's painful to see people constantly masking these wonderful traits. Of course, there's an etiquette we subscribe to in a professional setting, but that's not meant to turn you into a beige machine. It's meant to guide you about the expected behaviour in a particular workplace.

> Oh what tangled webs we weave when first we practice to deceive.
>
> **—Sir Walter Scott**

In Shakespeare's play *As You Like It*, there's a famous speech that begins 'All the world's a stage.' The character Jaques goes through stages of life, and when he talks about the professional, he does so in the context of a soldier who is 'jealous in honour'. Shakespeare meant that the soldier held honour dearly to his heart. Honour (integrity, authenticity) in business is not as widespread as we'd like, and Shakespeare's following two lines may explain why:

Seeking the bubble reputation
Even in the cannon's mouth.

I love that term: 'bubble reputation'. Basically, inflated and full of hot air. Shakespeare goes further, though. Even in the midst of peril (the cannon's mouth), this silly bubble stubbornly remains. This bubble is our ego. It sells itself as being our great protector, but it's rarely of positive help. People try and see your humanity through the bubble, but the bubble contorts it and makes it look like some weird reflection you would see in those funny mirrors at funfairs that make you look ridiculous.

We all have faults and fall short of whatever normal is, it's just that some people are better at hiding their failings, that's all.

The problem with the facade I've just described is that a false humility is only displayed when they want something, usually to those with more power. You might think no one can see this game, but don't be so sure. In fact, let me be frank: if the above describes you, everyone can see your act. How? Because 'everyone' is doing exactly the same as you. We all trip up, make mistakes, want to cry, laugh at stupid stuff, and want to reach out to those less fortunate, but the fake facade will not allow you to, and the toxic kinetic energy caused by this woeful to and fro will cause you inner dis-ease.

So, be humble or be humiliated. You may have experienced 'that' look you'll get from someone who sees right through you. All the world may be a stage, and yes, we've all put a front on now and then, but accepting yourself as you are and committing to exploring your true values and ambitions will give you the ability to have somewhere to hang your wholeheartedness. Brené Brown described her journey to embracing her vulnerability as a 'street fight', so roll your sleeves up. She said this 'you either walk inside your story and own it or you stand outside your story and hustle for your worthiness.'

Mickey Rourke's face tells you he's been in a few scrapes and had a few scraps in his time. The above is a quote of his, referring to fellow boxer Michael Bentt, who never actually wanted to be a boxer. In a documentary called *Losers* (Duzyj, 2019), Michael describes a horrific relationship with his pushy father. A dad who completely dismissed Michael's wishes as a boy, was detached as a father and disregarded his son's heart-wrenching pleas for mercy. The consequence of this and a lot of other parental behaviours (often nowhere near as extreme as what I've just shared) is what John Firman and Ann Gila describe as the primal wound from their ground-breaking book of the same name (Firman & Gila, 1997). When I read this book, I was profoundly moved.

> You can have all the talent in the world, but if you don't have somebody looking after your best interests, you're fu@ked.
>
> **—Mickey Rourke**

Primal wounds often come about during infancy. As children, many of us learned to lock away our true, core selves. Most parents are nowhere near as bad as Bentt's father, but they're still not as emotionally intelligent as they could be. They try their best, but dodgy parental practices are passed down the generations even if we promise never to be like our parents. With busy parents trying their best but not having the time or inclination to truly discover their authentic selves, never mind nurture even basic emotional proficiency, their children don't stand a chance. Think about the primal wound of abandonment. As babies, this is life-threatening. If we are abandoned, we die. Therefore, we have a built-in primal desire to do everything in our power not to be abandoned. We cry, look cute, or scream the house down not to be forgotten and potentially abandoned. I have seen the exact same behaviour in professionals!

Even with the best intentions, our caregivers displayed some shade of apathy which we saw as threatening to our very survival.

As a response we formed a false persona to meet the required rules of engagement that satisfied our guardians. Michael Bentt got beaten up professionally for it, I performed, and others receded into themselves. The consequence was a false survival personality that 'protected' the primal wound. As we grew older and interacted with others, some kind, some cruel, we learned to suppress genuine feelings and develop a false self to cope in this crazy world of mixed messages. However, as professionals, if we're going to make a genuine attempt at trusting ourselves and each other, this false self is no longer fit for purpose.

Although understandable, by creating this false persona we actually did ourselves a massive disservice. We enacted the biggest betrayal to our authentic selves. We detached from the authentic to survive. The ultimate act of apathy that propelled us into a place where survival of this false persona was paramount to protect our primal wound. As we became adults, we learned to bury ourselves in work, play, booze, food, sex, and status. But no matter how successful we became, there was still a dis-ease—a sense of not enough. Our false self cannot be satisfied as it suffers from the need for 'more'. It's in protection mode after all and will stockpile at all costs as danger feels imminent. So, many of us worked harder, played harder, or receded from our dreams. This becomes our reality, but when we pondered the universe on a starry night or looked deep into a baby's eyes, that awe gave us an indication that this false self was meaningless. There was something more profound within and around us.

We need to join the revolution at work that encourages us to break free from our false selves and connect authentically with ourselves and others. This is where our true power resides—not in a false self. Brene Brown and Johann Hari have written compelling books around this subject. Please check them out. Let's stop numbing our false selves so our authentic selves can get some 'time out'. Don't waste time trying to mentor or nurture fakeness. At work, create psychological safety and nurture connected relationships to propagate the authentic in all of us. You'll find true fulfilment from being more authentically you. The true you is magnificent.

I know this is deep. But if we're to get serious about nurturing ourselves and others, let's at least admit to what's really going on and stop pretending that something like putting doughnuts in the office is going to sort this out.

Learn this: Whatever you see outside comes from inside.

Everything happens for a reaction. It's cause and effect. How we react to the external is infused with our own perspectives of life before it's propelled back to the outside. This is our experience of life. Therefore, the above quote couldn't be truer. And remember what I said earlier: 'You don't see life as it is, you see life as you are.' Trust me, nothing is enough until you truly connect to the person you were always meant to be.

How are you? Do you know? The instant response is 'I'm fine', but are you? Do you know who you really are? Nurturing ourselves begins with being responsible for your own EQ, which focuses on self-awareness and relationships with others. This helps you consider how you see yourself and others. It also enables you to have a better relationship with yourself and others.

Seek to get in touch with your true essence. It takes some work. I've been to therapy, and I spend every day doing some form of mindfulness practice, and day by day, I feel more confident for you to see me. Not the false self's facade but me in all my vulnerability. The journey from a sense of not being seen (because of presenting a false version of myself) to getting in touch with self-love and empathy has been (and continues to be) the biggest journey of my life. Instead of accepting your false self that generates deep dissatisfaction and suffering, explore the possibility of true wholeheartedness by examining self-love and empathy.

And what does all this have to do with mentoring or work in general? *Everything!* If you're not providing psychological safety, you fan the flame of fake. If you encourage false self-coping mechanisms, you end up with teams who are undernourished and disconnected.

Feeding the false self is like eating gravy all your life. Instead, seek to mentor a tribe built on nurturing self-love and empathy, where you truly have each other's backs and where you celebrate success.

Nurturing Self

You are your worst nightmare and your greatest hope. Are you kind to yourself? When was the last time you did something for you, something nurturing, like making the effort to light some candles around your bath or buying yourself something really nice that you treasure? I'm not talking about something that's on a whim or an act that'll blot out the 'bad'. I'm talking about decompressing. Kindness to oneself is a great gauge to understand what you think of yourself. If you're not nurturing your body, mind, emotions or spirit, then you can't expect to be any good at nurturing others. Nurturing is not just a moment. It's a mindset.

Are you giving yourself time to re-energise? Walking in nature is my top tip. I live by Hampstead Heath in London on purpose. Going there is like a carwash for the soul. Making sure you're not lonely is also super important. I'm not talking about being in a crowd or being given some charity time by someone. I mean mutually beneficial relationships with others. Find interest groups on apps like Meetup. Take up a course on a subject that interests you, and you can meet other like-minded individuals. All these things will nurture you, bringing your energy up and your empathy out.

> Emotional self-awareness is the building block of the next fundamental emotional intelligence: being able to shake off a bad mood.
>
> —**Daniel Goleman (author of** *Emotional Intelligence***)**

If those with little EQ experience anger, they will react with anger. Angry people attract anger. If, however, we have EQ, we are able to discern that the angry person's anger is not our anger, we react differently and curtail the cycle of anger within us and, therefore, in the world around us. When I see anger, I actually see it as badly expressed pain. And look at issues like resentment: even though you're resentful of someone else, all the pain resides within you because it's you who has concocted the poison and it's you who's drinking it! There's an old saying. If you're going to dole out revenge, dig two graves.

Nurturing Others at Work

I want you to help your team to become more responsible for their own welfare. If they are coming to work tired because they like to indulge a little too much in the evening, then you need to talk. The workplace is not a rehab for late-night jollies. I'm not impressed with regular hangovers at work. You're paid to pay attention, not recover from the night before.

Remember that these conversations must be seeped in empathy. Listen carefully to what the team member is saying so you can truly understand. If you have to have these kinds of conversations, it's a good idea to make it clear that you are not a schoolteacher; they are adults and have the ability to make a choice. The choices they make, however, have consequences. You cannot rescue people. That's not empathy. If your team members are telling you they have lost the power of choice with booze, sleep, or anything of that nature, refer them to a doctor. You're not a medical professional.

I encourage my team members to get some fresh air during their day. The old saying 'move a muscle, change a thought' is spot on. They return with a reinvigorated body and mind. It doesn't take a genius to conclude that their work will also be rejuvenated!

Tools: Coaches and Mentors

1. Use the GROW model to navigate coaching interventions.
2. Put together a PDP (Personal Development Plan) with your team member. Ask about their ambitions at work over the next 1,3 and 5 years. Compile a PDP that reflects those ambitions. Build regular learning and development opportunities in the workplace. Show your team members you mean business around authenticity by working on yourself and share with them the books you've read and the courses you've taken to develop yourself.
3. Find your authentic self in the malaise of your false facades. Nurturing fake doesn't work.

ENERGY

The second domain is *energy*.

If you don't go within, you'll go without; and these next three disciplines are the power behind the light. The psychologist Carl Jung famously said, 'Who looks outside, dreams. Who looks inside, awakes.' These three disciplines help you to become an inner astronaut with the ability to navigate a path to increase performance in yourself and others.

The **ENERGY DOMAIN** disciplines:

> *Psychological Safety*
> *Seeks Deeper Connection*
> *Celebrates Success*

Psychological Safety

For you, your team and the business to be successful, your people do need to be reaching into the uncomfortable. It's essential they feel it's OK to innovate and create, to own stuff and make decisions. Now some of their decisions may not work out well but they must fundamentally grasp that the culture of the organisation will back them and not blame and shame. Remember, your overriding negativity bias sees threat from all corners, which is simply opposite to the environment we want to create. In Michael Bungay Stanier's excellent book *The Coaching Habit,* he writes, 'Five times a second, at an unconscious level, your brain is scanning the environment around you and asking itself: is it safe here or is it dangerous?' Need I say more? OK, just in case you haven't got it yet—it is critical to the success of the team to stay mindful about conscious empathy and be resolute about manifesting a culture of safety, not fear.

One great way to understand psychological safety is to think about abseiling. Without a rock-solid safety anchor and a strong rope that's been double-checked by an expert, would you really transfer your weight onto the rope and hang over the abyss? Of course not! If your team doesn't feel safe and secure, then there will be little trust or genuine cooperation. Creativity and innovation will be impaired, and high performance will be short-lived. So, make sure you're providing that safety and not expecting them to abseil using some telephone wire tied to a twig!

> Psychological safety in the workplace is one of the best predictors of high team performance.
>
> **—David Brendel, MD, PhD (Oesch, 2018)**

Check out Simon Sinek's book *Leaders Eat Last* (Sinek, Leaders Eat Last: Why Some Teams Pull Together and Others Don't, 2018), or his TED Talk 'How to Be a Great Leader' (TED, Simon Sinek: How Great Leaders Inspire Action | TED Talk, 2009). He describes a 'circle of safety'. Safety and security are the *fundamental* motivators of a high-performance culture. To me this is common sense, but believe me, it's not that common! Surely any person who genuinely cares for another person would want their environment to be one that is safe. Safe does not mean comfortable. They are two different things. In the context of a workplace, 'safe' means no threat or intimidation. No demoralisation or shaming, no humiliation or vitriol, and of course, no bullying or harassment. Being safe allows teams to reach into the uncomfortable. We create psychological safety to encourage innovation and great work. Not to wallow in the comfortable and fall asleep at the wheel.

Most of us are somewhat familiar with Maslow's hierarchy of needs (McLeod, 2018). This energy domain is basically Maslow, abridged.

- Safety needs – Psychological safety
- Belonging needs – Seek deeper connection
- Esteem needs – Celebrating success

Here is Maslow's hierarchy of needs in black and white: if you don't get the safety needs right, then anything else above them will not be able to fully materialise.

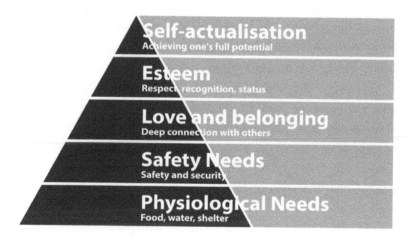

I think companies bizarrely expect all humans to rock up to their workplace with the bottom three needs intact and sorted. Friends, this is so naive. It shows little understanding of the state of humans and humanity. Your employees are seeking consistent clarity around safety needs. Don't think about a recognition program until there is psychological safety. For example, an online poll on UK stress levels conducted by YouGov, with 4,619 respondents, found that in the past year, 74 per cent of people have felt so stressed, they have been overwhelmed or unable to cope (Mental Health Foundation, n.d.). Businesses simply dismiss this and drive on thinking it won't affect performance. And who are the people left to sort out this woe? Yep, often ill-equipped managers!

One story I often share to illustrate psychological safety is about a small woodland in rural Cambodia. Down a dusty road, Noh, Nah, and their two children walk home with baskets overflowing with mushrooms. For a precious few weeks a year, these delicate white fungi can be harvested and sold at market—earning the family up to $100. With few prospects for permanent work, the family are reliant on what the land near their home can provide. The mushroom harvest is an opportunity Noh and Nah cannot afford to miss if they are to survive but foraging here comes at a risk. The notorious K5 barrier minefield runs across the land, threatening the lives of the villagers. Many have lost limbs, others have died trying to make ends meet, but the mushrooms are so valuable they feel there is little choice but to take the risk.

However, the family can now forage safely. Thanks to the amazing work of the HALO Trust, the landmines have been cleared—all of which could have killed or caused terrible injuries (The HALO Trust, n.d.). Next year, when the rains and mushrooms come, Noh, Nah, and the other villagers will be able to gather their precious harvest without fear. Productivity will soar because *they trust the land on which they tread.*

That story made me think about the workplace. On the surface of many a business I visit, all seems well, but dig a little, and you'll detect something more sinister. Do certain personalities make you wary about how carefully you have to tread in your workplace in case they detonate? These people create an atmosphere of little psychological safety. Do not expect high performance in a workplace riddled with threat!

Here are some other tips to create psychological safety:

- Acknowledge your mistakes.
- Break the golden rule and treat others the way they'd like to be treated.
- Encourage 'silly' questions.
- Approach conflict as a collaborator, not as an adversary.
- Stick up for a teammate in the face of adversity.
- Promote effectiveness not just efficiency. (explained in 'results driven')
- Lead by example by choosing empathy over apathy.
- Listen more (use the ARC technique).
- Ask team members to playback what you've just said.
- Create a culture of feedback using the 4X Model.
- Learn and use the drama triangle.

Also, think about the physical environment. Is it safe? Is it a place that feels more like a prison than a workplace? I consulted with one company where the 'boss' had a lovely, airy office with plants, coffee-making facilities, and awards glinting in the sunshine. Her team were stuck in a windowless office with boxes everywhere. She wondered why they were disengaged. Sometimes I just have to sigh quietly. Just be careful on this one though. Don't expect that if you sort out someone's office, they're going to become super engaged. I want you to really understand the cause and effect of psychological safety. Psychological safety fundamentally comes from the top of the organisation and the resulting engagement/ motivation of team members is an effect. It's not always *the* effect. It's not that simple. Remember, humans are complex, but I guarantee you that by understanding the cause and effects of psychological safety more clearly, you'll be able to significantly build trust to increase performance. Let's look at the effect using some classic motivational models.

Herzberg's Motivational Theory

No management program would be worth its salt without mentioning the psychologist Herzberg. He demonstrated that some positive responses to dissatisfaction don't make people satisfied, just less dissatisfied (Wikipedia, n.d.). This explains a lot. How many times have you given someone exactly what they wanted at work only to find that it didn't make them any more engaged, and after a couple of weeks they were back to their negative selves? You may have nurtured a workplace that is psychologically safe but there remains a whiff of disengagement or lack of motivation. Well, Herzberg's theory is sometimes called 'the two-factor theory' because he separates factors into two areas: hygiene and motivational factors.

Hygiene	Motivational
• Company policies • Rate of pay • Working conditions	• Personal growth • Recognition • Achievement

What Herzberg asserts is that you must get the hygiene factors right if you can, but don't expect them to motivate; they just make the team member less dissatisfied. For example, a team member has a bad back and you buy them a more comfortable chair. Yes, they will be less dissatisfied, but they will not be satisfied. So sure, sort out the hygiene factors, but also consider the motivational factors. Another example: a team member wants a pay rise and you give it to them. They may well become less dissatisfied for a time; however, if you now implement motivational factors like recognition for the work they've done by, say, giving public praise (celebrating success), you'll find that the team member will become satisfied.

I love Herzberg, please embrace his work. I'll never forget one coachee I worked with early in my career. It was a steep learning curve and a great example of Herzberg. I asked how they were feeling out of one hundred? They said around 30 per cent. I replied that 30 per cent was awfully low, and they explained two reasons. Firstly, they had back pain and wanted a special chair. Secondly, they had asked if they could use some holiday leave but no one had got back to them. So, I put on my superman cape and got to work. I made the case for an ergonomic chair and sorted out the holiday dates. I remember it being a massive drain on my time. The company spent several hundred pounds on a chair that NASA would have been proud of. A short time passed and I caught up with the coachee. I said, 'Last time we spoke you were at 30 per cent. Now you have an amazing chair, and you have the holiday dates. What's your percentage now?' My mouth hit the floor when she said, 'Oh, around 35 per cent!'

> Don't be led by sight, be led by insight.
>
> **—Nara Lee**

A lack of psychological safety can make people close down and not be open to change or growth. A bit like a tortoise shooting its head back into its shell when it senses danger. Please make public moves to show that the environment is safe. You may be dealing with team members who have a fixed mindset. They are going to be tricky to bring out of their 'safe' shell, but we must encourage growth mindsets at work, and that starts with psychological safety and then motivation.

Growth or Fixed Mindset

There's a very clear difference between a fixed and a growth mindset, and that's an intention to learn. Encouraging a fixed mindset to learn can feel like trying to get a child to eat Brussels sprouts. Their mouth is firmly closed, and often their eyes are shut too. Just saying that they have to eat their greens doesn't make it any more appealing.

Fixed mindsets may come from previous experience in the workplace which led to psychological unsafety and therefore closing down. At work the answer is to show them, not tell them. Help team members see the advantages of a growth mindset by enjoying and not enduring any learning intervention. Also, think about discovering this at the interview stage. What have they learned recently? This is a great question to unearth those who are either too important to learn, just too lazy or have experienced psychological unsafety. A growth mindset is a state of mind, so if your mind is in a state, it's not going to be easy to be open to learning. Mindfulness can also really help here.

> You're as happy as you make your mind up to be.
>
> **—Abraham Lincoln**

Get your team into a habit of learning. Here are some practical suggestions:

- A monthly TED Talk where everyone comes and watches and then discusses. Thirty minutes of learning.
- 121s. Reading a book together.
- If someone goes on a course, get them to report back to the team about what learnings they picked up.

Intrinsic versus Extrinsic Motivation

Intrinsic motivation involves doing something because it's personally rewarding to you. You'll experience some inner satisfaction. Extrinsic motivation is about doing something because you want to get a reward or avoid punishment from an external source.

Here are some examples:

Subject	Intrinsic	Extrinsic
Pay for job		X
Passion for job	X	
Learning	I love learning new things.	I get a promotion if I learn this.
Wellbeing	I look after myself because it makes me feel better.	I don't want others to judge my appearance.

It's good to expect a healthy balance between both extrinsic and intrinsic, but if it's weighted too heavily on just extrinsic motivators, then you'll find the team member will never be truly happy. So, in your day-to-day encounters with team members, encourage intrinsic motivators like the following:

- Curiosity
- Celebration
- Enjoyment

My experience has shown me that those motivated by only extrinsic motivators never care as much as those with intrinsic motivators. For those galvanised by pure extrinsic motivation like pay, power, or prestige, sometimes you'll find them suffering from chronic dissatisfaction as motivators like a pay increase soon wear off. Once again, look out for intrinsic motivation at their interview, and if it becomes a problem in the workplace, help your team member understand the difference between these two states and encourage some self-exploration about what truly makes them happy. Don't be surprised if psychological safety is mentioned.

> If people are good only because they fear punishment, and hope for reward, then we are a sorry lot indeed.
>
> **—Albert Einstein**

There's a lot to consider when it comes to the causes and effects of psychological safety but be sure of this, sort out the cause and you won't have to deal with the effect! Before we move onto the next discipline, one behaviour that can really affect psychological safety is how consistent you are.

When I was talking about this book to other professionals, I asked them what built trust from their experience. Consistency was mentioned over and over again. Many spoke about the worst managers they've had, and all of them mentioned a lack of consistency. Now, if you're getting feedback that you're a Jekyll-and-Hyde character, go and see a therapist and challenge that behaviour. Don't let others suffer because of your pain. Hurt people will hurt people, so it's important that any emotional distress that you're leaking into the workplace is addressed.

> Trust is built with consistency.
>
> **—Lincoln Chafee**

Please don't have favourites. Team members' antennae are highly tuned to favouritism and it never ends well. Make sure each one of your team is getting the same amount of attention, care, and support. If you've worked with one individual longer than others, you're going to have to have a conversation. Decent peeps will understand that relationships change. Consistency is all about being fair. Always remember: do what is right, not what is easy.

Inconsistent managers may well have inconsistent leaders. Please stop being so passive to these people. Diplomatically address your concerns around mixed messages or frequent changes of direction.

Great leaders listen, and you'll soon get a feel for whether they need to read this book or not. Your team members need dependability in an uncertain world. The outside environment (market conditions, political decisions, etc.) creates enough weather to deal with, so please don't let your managers or yourself add to it.

Consistency allows for some really important things. It creates accountability, something that is so often forfeited due to fickleness or impulsivity. And consistency means you can truly measure success. If you don't stick to a strategy, you'll never really know if it is going to work or not. Hold firm to your goals, and don't let a blip, torpedo your business.

> Consistency is the DNA of mastery.
>
> —Robin Sharma

The best way that I have built consistency is through my mindfulness practice. At the start of each day, I make a mindful choice to enjoy rather than endure my day. I commit to thinking of others rather than myself. When I get in the office, I make a plan for the day. I schedule in time to GSD (get sh!t done). I make sure my days are not crazily back to back, and I also make time for my team.

Here are some tips around consistency:

1. If people are feeding back that you're Jekyll and Hyde, see a therapist.
2. Consistency in practice gives you awesome parameters to measure, so stick with a strategy for at least three months so you can objectively see if it works.
3. Work is more like a marathon but often run in bursts of sprints, so make sure your team is not sprinting at different times. Unify the pace.

Tools: Psychological Safety

1. Use the tips to increase psychological safety and think of Maslow's hierarchy of needs. This domain is basically Maslow, abridged.
2. Be mindful of Herzberg's motivational theory and understand the difference between hygiene and motivational factors.
3. Get some 360 feedback on yourself. Are you being consistent? If not, why not? Go see a therapist if you need some issues resolving and don't take it out on the team.

Seeks Deeper Connection

Listening

I had to learn to listen. As I have matured, listening has become more and more important. Everybody has a deep desire to be heard. This is a fundamental practice that is crucial for you to develop. In

> When others feel heard by you they're more likely to listen to you.
>
> **—Roger Fisher and William L. Ury,** *Getting to Yes*

fact, there was an occasion that really grounded me to how dismissive we can be about this critical element of communication. I was in a meeting with a conference organiser. We were discussing a speech I was about to make in the coming weeks.

'So, Mr Davies,' she said, full of intrigue, 'have you decided what gem of business acumen you'll bestow? What golden nugget you're going to furnish this esteemed audience with?'

She giggled to herself, pleased with her prose-like questioning. She waited with bated breath, and I, not one to break the anticipatory atmosphere, paused, dramatically leant forward, and said, 'Listening.'

Her jaw uncoupled from her face and hit the floor. As if momentarily concussed by my words, she replied slowly, loudly and with disbelief, '*Listening?*' I winced a little as she gasped, concerned that she was about to lynch me. Luckily, she just shook her head and said, 'Darling, these are top executives from around the world who will have flown in for an internationally renowned conference, and you're going to lecture them on ...' she found it really hard to say the word, 'liiiiiiissssstttttening?'

'Yes,' I said. She paused, gathering her thoughts. 'Matthew, sweetie,' she began, trying the softly-softly approach, 'these people are Harvard and Oxford graduates on six-figure salaries. Can you choose something more ...' fighting for the right word, she finally blurted out, 'something more complex.'

A Steve Jobs quote surfaced in my head: 'Simple can be harder than complex: you have to work hard to get your thinking clean to make it simple. But it's worth it in the end because once you get there, you can move mountains.'

You've probably heard of active listening, but do you practise it? I will never get tired of quoting the top book on negotiating, *Getting to Yes* (Fisher & Ury, 2012). I especially love this sentence, so I'll say it again: 'When others feel heard by you, they're more likely to listen to you.' In one little sentence, the gateway to better relationships is beautifully articulated. However, we are determined to do the opposite, and as mentioned earlier, 'Most people do not listen with the intent to understand. Most people listen with the intent to reply.'

Therefore, do not underestimate the power of listening—I mean, *really* listening, or as it's called in the business, 'active listening'. When you listen actively, you are demonstrating that you value the other person's voice. It shows that what they are saying is just as important as what you are saying, indicating that you care. This takes time to master, because frankly, we're all a bit too self-obsessed and think we're right most of the time.

Active listening requires a healthy dose of humility. Now, I'm not looking for some pious grovelling; that's not humility. As I learned once, humility isn't 'thinking less of yourself'; it's 'thinking of yourself less'. You don't always know best, you don't always guess right about where a conversation is going, you do make mistakes, and you have cocked up many times. In fact, I'd go as far as to say, 'Be humble or be humiliated.' Not my line but definitely my experience. More on that later. Humility is the cornerstone of active listening, so as my Irish mother used to say, 'Count yourself; you're not that many!' Apathy is the best earplug. Therefore, take action to overcome this insidious characteristic.

Please practise your listening skills. I have devised a simple system called the listening 'ARC'.

It's an acronym for attend, register, and clarify.

1. **Attend:** Refocus out of the white noise and make a mindful decision to listen.
2. **Register:** Show them that you're listening. Write stuff down and use body language. Do not pre-empt or interrupt. Even if it's boring, let them have their say.
3. **Clarify:** Confirm and clarify by playing back what they've said and ask probing questions.

First, focus on what the other person is saying. There are plenty of extraneous distractions from construction work to other people speaking loudly on their phones. Simply focus in on the conversation you wish to listen to. There are also internal distractions from feeling hungry to an overthinking mind wandering off to another topic. Leave all that at the door and simply focus on what the other person is saying. This is where mindfulness practice pays off as you can truly pay attention.

Second, show the person that you're listening by writing stuff down and nodding. I am always amazed when participants come to class and bring nothing to write down with. How on earth are they going to remember? It's a real indicator that they don't know how to learn or listen. Do not pre-empt or interrupt. Allow someone to say what they have to say. Only if they begin to repeat themselves can you gently steer them. By interrupting or pre-empting, you are showing them who's boss, who's in control. That's not what great managers do. We learn to listen and then listen to learn.

Finally, clarify by summarising what the other person is saying. Summarising is vital to be clear that what you heard is what they meant. It's a good idea not to overlook this step. Even if you get some part wrong, it actually shows that you care to get it right! So smartly summarise (rather than repeat word for word) and corroborate what they have said. Finally, ask them some questions. What they meant to say and what they actually said can be quite different, so elucidate with fervour.

I also believe listening is the cornerstone of having a growth mindset. If you have a fixed mindset, why would you genuinely pay attention to others? Paying attention is about being open to what is right in front of you. You must have been in a situation, maybe at a networking event, where someone was speaking at you but looking over your shoulder. Inside, I wish them good grace on their travels as they soon scuttle off to someone more 'important'. How can you grow if you're not listening? You definitely need a growth mindset for change. This starts with listening.

There have been some amazing downfalls as a result of not listening. Take the Kodak story (Pangarkar, 2012). They were a mega-company in the 70s and 80s with hundreds of thousands of staff and an awesome mission: 'You press the button and we'll do the rest.' We'd send our camera film to them, and they'd transform our memories into treasured technicolour photographs that we'd hang up in our front rooms and beside our beds to remember happy times. This brand had a place in our souls! Oh, to have a brand with that much connection to its customers! It had financial clout and was developing digital cameras in the mid-1970s. So, what went wrong? Commentators say they had too much of an inward focus. They knew best, but they didn't, and within a few years, they had a workforce of around only six thousand and a hell of a mountain to climb. They didn't listen! They didn't pay attention—I mean *really* pay attention—to what was happening around them.

Your silence does not indicate consent or agreement. It shows that you desire to understand before being understood. Once people know that you have heard them, believe me, they will listen to you.

> The word LISTEN contains the same letters as the word SILENT.
>
> **—Alfred Brendel**

> Listen thrice
>
> Think twice
>
> Speak Once
>
> **—Author unknown**

The ability to actively listen is essential to your success as a manager, indeed as a human. Effective communication starts with your mouth shut!

121s

These are not catchups, coaching sessions or an arena to talk shop. 121s are moments where you connect and mentor your team member. Let me make the case for these critical encounters. You *must* have regular one-on-one time with each of your team members. No excuses.

Remember when you were a child. It wasn't just how much money your parents gave you; it was how much meaningful time they spent with you, right? Same at work. You must have regular one-on-one time with each of your team members. No excuses. I want you to implement this immediately. Upto sixty minutes every fortnight. That's only two hours a month, one day a year, to take time out to be empathic and encourage connection. If that's not possible just a 30-minute walk out of the office to get a coffee will do. We do not use 121s as a place for pent-up problem solving; they are a place to nurture human connection by listening, understanding, getting to know someone, and letting them get to know you. Talk openly about your family. Encourage them to do the same. Remember their kids' and dogs' names!

Be interested and not just interesting. All this builds connection and therefore makes collaboration thrive. Remember: connection, then trust, then collaboration. Apathetic managers fail in this. They either waffle on about work or cancel at a moment's notice, clearly signalling that their staff are not important in the pecking order.

You may worry that you won't have anything to talk about, or you may genuinely be put off by what's called 'small talk'. Small talk is a critical and highly undervalued skill. Hear me out on this. Have you ever wondered what small talk really is? It's a way to determine whether you're going to feel OK about connecting with someone. It's the human equivalent of a dog smelling another dog's butt. Small talk settles us into a deeper conversation and says, 'I'm OK. You're OK. It's OK to get closer.'

This is what I'm looking for from you as a result of 121s with your team members—a genuine and keen understanding of their lives. You need to get to know a team member and be interested in their life. There's an old saying: 'If you knew everything about someone, you'd instantly forgive them.' Understanding more about someone's current and past situation helps put lots of behaviours into context.

As a test, do you know:

- Their partner's name and a little about them?
- Where they live?
- Their close family circumstances?
- Their hobbies?
- If they have any health issues?
- What makes them laugh?
- How they like to be communicated with?

Apathetic managers don't know the names of their team member's family. Empathic managers have met the family. You could both agree to read an inspirational book (I've mentioned many in this book) and talk about it in your 121s. Please do not underestimate the value of this time. You may have obvious roles and be brought together by work, but 'a hidden connection is stronger than an obvious one', as Heraclitus of Ephesus said.

Some top tips:

- Go for a walk and talk or go to a cafe for a coffee; 121s are not formal occasions.
- These are not moments to give constructive feedback but places where your team member can talk about their struggles around relationships and feedback they're receiving or giving from colleagues.
- Stay curious and probe answers so you get a deep understanding of their circumstances.

I read this somewhere: 'Understanding is deeper than knowledge.' There are many people who know you but few who understand you. Empathy is the ability to connect and understand rather than just be understood. We use 121s as the place to help you connect and understand your team members and for them to connect and understand you too.

A word of caution. Introverts take longer to open up than extroverts. Do not push introverts to open up. They will open up but at their own pace. I heard somewhere that asking an introvert to open up is like asking an extrovert to shut up. So take it easy with introverts. They will open up but in their own time.

For those new to 121s, here's a step-by-step guide on how to do it.

121s Step-By-Step Guide

1. Don't be late or regularly cancel.
2. Ask them how they are between 1 and 100 per cent. (Ask this every time and refer to previous scores.) Enquire both sides of the score. For example, if they say 70 per cent, dig deeper about the reasoning behind the 70 per cent (Whoop-whoop! Celebrate success) and then dig down into the reasons for the 30 per cent that's missing. (Listen intently. *Do not give advice.* Just listen using the ARC technique described earlier). Do not rescue. (Remember the Drama Triangle).
3. Follow up on how things went from the previous 121. Show them that you heard, remembered, and care.
4. Open up about your week, but do not dominate the time. This is *their* time. So, think about using up five minutes tops about your challenges at work *and at home.*
5. Decide on a book to read together. Each time you meet, talk about a chapter and what you've learned.
6. Find something you're both passionate about and share that together.
7. Make sure that you're not spoon-feeding them through 121s. It's important they bring stuff to talk about for 121s. I ask my team members to bring a topic or a concern to 121s.
8. Encourage learning. Ask them to bring evidence of stuff they've learned. Share your learnings. This will aid their professional development which is critical to keep team members engaged.

Questioning

Many managers flounder in 121s because they're not being curious enough. You need to learn the art of asking open questions. Interviewing when recruiting is a powerful place to learn questioning techniques. Let's look at questioning in the context of hiring as a way of bringing some context to this section.

There are two steps needed to be an excellent questioner. Firstly, ask open questions. Secondly, probe deeply. You'll find this problem everywhere in your communications with colleagues, especially others who are addicted to apathy. They'll ask a question and not follow up, *or* worse, they'll just ask a closed question in the hope of a quick answer so they can move on with their agenda. Connect, friends! Use open questioning and probing to take a deep dive to get some valuable insight.

Once you've asked the initial open question, the key is to dig deeper and probe on what they've just told you. In life, we skim. Social media has made us accustomed to flying through data without really digging deeper. We believe the newspaper headline without reading the full article and don't have time to really investigate *all* the facts. This is happening in 121s and the hiring room. Managers are asking closed questions which reveal little. So, start asking open questions. Here's the difference. Firstly, closed questions:

> You: 'So you worked at ABC Company?'
> Them: 'Yes.'
> You: 'In customer success?'
> Them: 'Yes.'

Do I need to go on? Inexperienced interviewers then start to freak out because they run out of questions really quickly and haven't revealed anything about the candidate. Try it this way:

> You: 'What did you love about ABC Company?'
> Them: 'My work colleagues were fantastic.'
> You: 'All of them?'
> Them: Talks about disliking the new line manager.

You: 'So your new line manager was the reason you left? Can you give me an example of a time when they really messed up for you?'

Them: Extensive answer.

You: Probe that answer. This is where you get the big fish. After some probing, you may discover that your candidate was overlooked for the (line manager) role that the new person got. She actually became resentful and left. All this raises questions about *why* she was overlooked.

I hope you can see why probing is essential. Asking open questions and then probing also demonstrates curiosity; you're showing that you're interested rather than trying to be interesting. Please practise open questions if you sincerely seek a deeper connection.

Tools: Seeks Deeper Connection

1. Talk less, listen more. Use the ARC technique.
2. Be consistent with your 121s.
3. Embrace the power of small talk and use open questioning and probing techniques.

Celebrates Success

One attitude that really frustrates team members is the feeling that their efforts are never enough. We achieve goals and hurriedly move on to the next ones. It's time we paused and genuinely celebrated success. Recognition is not just in the paycheque. It's also up to managers to demonstrate their appreciation of team members' work. You can do this by simply saying well done to someone. You can encourage a time in company meetings to celebrate success. No buts, by the way. 'Well done, but ...' is bad practice. Stop it! Success celebrated is a moment when we recognise a good job. There are other times when we review projects in coaching sessions and meetings called 'retros' or 'wash-ups' that we can review, learn, and develop. They are different times to this. Success should be celebrated weekly, not once every six months. Doing this will also dispel any threat response the team member may feel, resulting in them lowering defences and accepting constructive feedback more easily.

I must thank my mate Tracy Paterson for this top tip regarding celebrating success. She started a monthly/quarterly 'wheel of wow'. I use it wherever I go. It's simple yet so much fun. Ask for nominations from team members for others who've gone the extra mile or done great work. Spin the wheel and allocate prizes. Have some fun prizes. You can also read out nominations then put them in a hat and pull out one as the winner. You're celebrating success and having some fun at the same time.

Paul Zak is a professor who has worked extensively on the neurobiology of trust. I love this guy! In his breakthrough book called *The Trust Factor. The science of creating high performance teams* (Zak, 2018) his findings match my experience. He calls celebrating success 'ovation' and has found in his research that it is a critical factor in building trust. Professor Paul has been around the world studying brain activity and the chemical changes around the theme of trust and I profoundly agree with his findings. I've written extensively in this book about understanding that team members are human beings and not human resources. Celebrating success is a fundamental principle for humans, remember our primary threat or reward response! Professor Paul says in his book that 'trust requires viewing those with whom one works as whole and complete human beings, not as human capital.' He noted that a Boston Consulting Group survey found that ovation is the most important thing colleagues want at work. By the way, in that same survey, salary was number eight on the list!

From a simple thank you to a program around recognition, please celebrate success in your business.

Tools: Celebrates Success

1. Create a Slack channel called kudos for instant celebration of success.
2. In your 121s make sure you have something to thank your team member for. If not, why not?
3. Use the wheel of wow.

EXPERTISE

> Humble enough to prepare, confident enough to perform.
>
> —Tom Coughlin

A quick word before we launch into this domain. I'm trained in the Myers-Briggs Type Indicator. Please check it out as many of my clients find this personality assessment to be hugely insightful. When setting clear expectations, some preferences will find it more natural than others. Those with a clear 'J' preference tend to have a natural propensity to plan, while those with a clear 'P' preference may feel that the expertise domain is restrictive. 'Ps' often prefer being emergent and going with the flow. I have also noticed that those with a clear 'N' preference can get quickly frustrated with the process of setting clear expectations and being evidence-based. They just want some top lines and no real detail. When communicating expectations 'Ns' can lose colleagues because their expectations can be too big picture and vague. Here, awareness is key. Remember, humans are complex, and your MBTI is not a label; it's insight! The good news is 'Ns' can turn up their 'S' and 'Ps' can raise their 'J' game. Just because you are a particular type does not mean you don't have the capacity to increase your 'out of preference' traits. You do it every day. If you get frustrated with this domain try working with others rather than struggling alone.

We all have different strengths and someone you know will love the idea of the nitty-gritty of planning.

Here are the three disciplines of the **EXPERTISE DOMAIN**:

Sets Clear Expectations
Evidence Based
Results Driven

The ultimate purpose of the expertise domain is to provide the right conditions for autonomy. My position is clear though: no accountability, no autonomy.

Sets Clear Expectations

So many professionals work in a murky world of not being clear about what's truly expected of them. Some people guess and then fall foul of managers who expect that their team members should mind-read. I know one guy who is consistently encouraged by his manager to do certain tasks that the wider company does not even remunerate him for. The parameters for his annual review do not take into consideration the work that he actually does, which is based around innovation. His company only pays him a bonus for selling the same old stuff. He's caught between the devil and the deep blue sea. Does he innovate and not receive a bonus, or does he sell the old stuff off the shelf and get the bonus? This is just one of many examples of the mess that can be created if you do not set clear expectations—not just for the individual but also for the team and the company.

Well-run companies have strategic alignment. It looks like this:

At the top are the company's objectives. Each part of the business works out how it can help the company hit those objectives. Notice the golden thread that runs all the way up and down. This is a good measure to ascertain if whatever a team member is doing is helping the common strategic goal. If it's not, why are they doing it?

Clear expectations are a road map for you and your team. It's really demotivating to be told that the work you've been doing for the last few days, weeks, or months is now useless. People are the most expensive asset of your business, so use their time wisely.

An exercise I do to demonstrate this is quite fun as well as illuminating: look around and note in your mind two objects that are red. Now close your eyes and tell me some objects you saw that are grey. When I did this, my brain was literally like a grumpy teenager: 'But you said red!' Thinking of grey objects was, frankly, annoying—especially with those red objects in my head! The point of the exercise is this: a clear expectation like 'find two red objects' has clarity, but change that mid-flow, and confusion breeds frustration, which, in turn, can easily morph into apathy. Clarity is key when setting expectations, but you must diagnose before you prescribe.

The first step in setting clear expectations is to define what the problem is. Steve Jobs said, 'If you define the problem correctly, you almost have the solution.'

What is the problem that you need to solve? Check out the '5 Whys' technique. This method can be used to define the root cause of the problem that can therefore clarify an expectation just as much as helping provide evidence. Feel free to use this for setting clear expectations as well as being evidence-based. The 5 Whys was developed by Sakichi Toyoda, a Japanese inventor and industrialist (MindTools, n.d.). The technique became an integral part of the Toyota philosophy, which says, 'The basis of Toyota's scientific approach is to ask 'why' five times whenever we find a problem. By repeating 'why' five times, the nature of the problem as well as its solution becomes clear.' The 5 Whys analysis has the purpose of assessing a certain problem in depth until it shows you the root cause. There are tons of resources online regarding the 5 Whys, so please dig in and enjoy.

The next step is to work out the pathway to solving that problem by setting clear expectations.

Set clear expectations with team members on a weekly, monthly, quarterly and yearly basis. This is a foundational task for managers, but many don't know how to, don't get the necessary info from their leaders, or just don't bother (apathy). It takes time to plan expectations. Impatient managers throw themselves into delivery without a clear road map. They end up someplace else from where they intended. Take a simple example like travelling from London up north to Manchester. Seems simple—that is definitely an expectation, but it's not clear.

Here's another tool. The five W's—why, what, when, who, and where (and a little tip: stick a 'how' in as well). In this example we've answered one of the W's. We know where we're going, but we still need to consider questions like the following:

- Why are we going there?
- What are we hoping to achieve?
- How are we getting there?
- When do we go?
- Who do we go with?

Fail to prepare, prepare to fail. Seems obvious, right? So obvious we miss it. Remember some of the simplest things in life are the most difficult to achieve. Look at weight loss. Eat less, exercise more—couldn't be simpler. Yet, most of us are lumbering around, baffled at our ever-expanding girths. Please take time to set clear expectations when managing people and processes. Can you answer the following four questions? Your answers must be specific.

1. What is the quantity of work expected?
2. What is the quality of work expected?
3. Are these expectations based on data or intuition?
4. Are these SMART expectations?

Clear expectations should not be a book. It's a good idea to make them a short, punchy document that is super clear. Using the SMART approach is a great way to set clear expectations.

SMART goals

Setting clear expectations is the most important contract between you and your employee you'll ever make. These expectations are clearly agreed upon and always referred to and reviewed in the weekly report. More about that later.

Please use SMART goals (CFI, n.d.). You may know what it stands for, but I bet you don't actually use this principle consistently. SMART goals are the building blocks for writing really great goals.

When you're setting expectations, double-check that the objectives you set yourself and your team pass the SMART goals test:

Specific   — Be really precise, not generic

Measurable — There <u>must</u> be a number attached

Attainable   — Can this be done? Stretch goals, but don't set unrealistic ones.

Relevant   — Is this a priority, and where does it sit in the scheme of all work?

Timely   — Gain absolute clarity on when this needs to be achieved.

Please apply SMART goals consistently. Where are these goals going to be stored? Write down tasks in an agreed Trello (Trello, n.d.), not endless emails or a messenger app where they can get lost.

Setting Expectations around Behaviour

I feel like weeping when I see teams displaying destructive consent (that's when team members do their job, but under their breath, they despise or disagree with how it's been set out). When asked, you'll get the 'I'm fine' response, but clearly, they're unhappy. They'll bitch and moan and play victim because they feel disempowered, neglected, or unheard. I once overheard a man on the train talking to his friend about the new dress code at work. 'From Monday,' he said, 'we've been told we must wear a suit, shirt, and tie.' He went on to say, 'Well, I'm going into Oxfam to buy the worst possible tie. F@$k 'em!' That, my friends, is destructive consent. There are many reasons for this mindset. From neglect and little meaningful connection to the team member not having the courage to leave when the 'sell by date' on their enthusiasm has expired. One issue I have also observed is not setting, and consistently re-enforcing, clear expectations around the sort of behaviour that is acceptable in the workplace. I've experienced younger team leads displaying immaturity because they're not clear about what their expected behaviours should be. So, allow to me spell that out. Professionalism is based in two areas, focus and etiquette. We are paid to pay attention and focus on work related activities in the professional environment. The second expectation is etiquette. We expect managers to be mature at work and not act like stroppy teenagers. If you're a young manager (under twenty-seven years old-ish), please take note. Some work cultures can seem very informal but that does not excuse behaviour that wouldn't be acceptable in a schoolyard. Please remember you're a role model to your team members, so act like one.

Try your best to work to encourage a culture of constructive dissent. This is where employees can respectfully disagree with good intent for the betterment of the business. Here, disgruntled employees feel their voice is being heard, and they can openly disagree for the greater good of the organisation.

Remember, never accept childish behaviour in any shape or form. Some of these people get off on destructive consent. If they show a real unwillingness to positively contribute to the organisation and start infecting the wider team, then set super-clear boundaries and if it persists, share the Skill Will Model and ask them which quadrant they think they're in.

Skill Will Model

This is a great tool to help counter destructive consent. It's called the Skill Will model, made popular by Max Landsberg and others (The Peak Performance Center, n.d.). This will help you determine, behaviourally, where your team member is and how to deal with them.

SKILL or WILL Model

The Cynic **MOTIVATE** Identify constraints Do not allow to Manage	**The Awesome Worker** **DELEGATE** Give additional responsibilty Collaborate on decisions
The Nervous Beginner **DIRECT** Instruct and guide clearly Watch out for threat responce	**The Enthusiastic Beginner** **GUIDE** Coach / Mentor Praise and Encourage

SKILL (vertical axis) — WILL (horizontal axis)

The cynic has usually been in the business for a while, and you can't tell them anything, whereas the nervous beginner is new and needs clear instructions. The enthusiastic beginner is usually pretty bright and learns quickly. We'd love the awesome worker to manage the enthusiastic beginner, but they're usually too busy. Please encourage the awesome worker to find time to work with the enthusiastic beginner, as it's imperative we get the newbies to spend time with the top performers and not those who could infect the newbies with cynicism. We need to discover the roots of the cynic's woes. Is it psychological safety or motivation?

Here are a few tips:

- Never allow an enthusiastic beginner to be coached by a cynic. They'll turn into one!
- The cynic was once an awesome worker. What happened? Can it be fixed? Time to go?
- Set clear expectations to the nervous beginner. Coach closely.

- Give plenty of time to the awesome worker. These people are the important workers and can easily be taken for granted.

Heartfelt Expectations

You can be as logical as you like, but when it comes to human beings, it's emotions that truly motivate. Trust is a feeling, not a thought.

That's why setting clear expectations is not about covering your back because you sent an email. It's on us, the team leaders, to create clear materials and make sure our teams *agree and understand*, but that's not enough. It's essential we nurture an environment that welcomes 'silly' questions.

'Sets clear expectations' is a great example of the necessity to provide psychological safety in the workplace in order for others to have the courage to reach out when they don't understand. If you rush through expectations, setting them 'at' and not 'with' team members, you could be inadvertently making matters worse! Not giving space for others to deeply understand the expectation and feel OK asking 'silly' questions will just make the individual close down because they may experience shame about feeling stupid. We *must* connect with team members and demonstrate through actions that it's OK to show vulnerability and not be afraid to ask *anything*. I encourage this wherever I go to the extent that we celebrate when someone feels OK to say they don't understand. This will build trust and model a behaviour, meaning more people feel OK to say that they're not OK. By the way, notice how many times I mentioned the word 'feel'. Emotions are five times stronger than rational thought (Peters, 2012), so miss out dealing with feelings and you end up in a soup of confusion with a defensive employee, closed down and turned off to any expectations. Hence the importance of working with team members on building out expectations, encouraging psychological safety and not dismissing if someone feels a certain way. If I hear a manager say 'you shouldn't feel like that' to a team member, I will personally throw a bucket of water over them (as empathically as possible). Thank team members for sharing and listen carefully to their concerns, unpicking the problem together to reach a solution that makes sense for both parties.

So, I hope you understand that setting clear expectations isn't 'job done' because you've written a weighty tome that's buried in Google Drive. The written word is a poor connector compared to the power of face to face. Trust grows through connection, and only then can true collaboration increase.

Make sure your intent is transparent. You're setting clear expectations not to control but to support and enrich autonomy. Setting clear expectations are agreements and not impositions.

Always ask team members to 'play back' the expectation so you can actually witness if they've got it. In training, we say 'you've only learned a lesson if you can pass it on to someone else'.

Setting Clear Expectations Using the Drawbridge

No relationship starts with deep trust, and in most relationships, trust levels ebb and flow depending on circumstances. I want you to understand this clearly by using the analogy of a drawbridge. I've defined the four stages of a relationship between a team member and a team leader based on Bruce Tuckman's model for team dynamics (MindTools, n.d.).

At which stage do you *really* think you are with your team member? Artificial harmony is generated when you're at an early stage but think you're further down the track. Please don't think trust is a one-way street. It ebbs and flows. You may be at stage four with a team member, and then something happens and you're back to stage two—that's unfortunate but not bad. It's how life breathes: two steps forward, one step back.

The drawbridge

Stage 1: Forming

Team Member
Listens and learns
Passive

**No connection
Total distrust**

Team Leader
Directive
Sets clear expectations

Stage 2: Storming

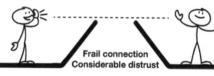

Team Member
Challenges
Less passive

**Frail connection
Considerable distrust**

Team Leader
Supervisor
Evidence based

Stage 3: Norming

Team Member
Agrees
Takes responsibility

**Connection manifests
Trust begins**

Team Leader
Guides
Results driven

Stage 4: Performing

Team Member
Autonomous

**Strong connection
Trusted relationship**

Team Leader
Delegates

Stage One Is Forming

Trust takes time to nurture, so when you're onboarding the team member, they need to ascertain whether this is a safe place. As the team leader, you need to nurture the relationship by first setting clear expectations about what's required for them to flourish. Notice the team leader is directive. This should only happen at the beginning of a relationship or if something goes wrong during it. Being directive should *not* be an overarching behaviour in the relationship. Back to the onboarding process. You're informing the team member, who is listening more than talking because they need to learn. At this point the drawbridge is up, and there is no trust and only a whiff of connection.

Stage Two Is Storming

The team member has now got an understanding of the role and responsibilities and may question why they are done that way. For a team leader with little emotional intelligence, this is difficult. They'll feel threatened and go into 'defend and control' mode. That makes the team member feel insignificant and not truly seen.

We need to encourage constructive dissent (allow and encourage reasonable challenge) with the team leader offering robust evidence for their reasoning while allowing the team member to challenge more. Done well, the drawbridge lowers, and a frail connection is formed even though there is still considerable distrust.

Stage Three Is Norming

Good team leaders work *with* their team. They do not impose. By now, the team member feels that they matter in the process, and after storming comes norming. Instead of being supervisory, the team leader guides the team member with super-clear results set.

Here, autonomy begins. Bad managers give autonomy away at stage one and wonder why distrust remains, and that's because it's only here in stage three that the team member can take real responsibility because they wholeheartedly agree. And because of that involvement, connection manifests as trust truly starts to flourish. Remember: no accountability, no autonomy.

Stage Four Is Performing

There is now a strong and trusted relationship, with the team leader feeling confident of delegating as clear expectations are set, evidence is accepted and both parties are results driven. This strong connection means performance increases.

Be sure of this, though: the drawbridge is not locked. If the team member fails in delivering, then the relationship may return to stage two. If there is an incident where trust is broken, the relationship may head all the way back to stage one. Do not kid yourself that trust is not a living, movable feast. Let trust breathe and be transparent with team members that it's your job to guide, supervise, or even direct if the circumstance arises. The message I want you to get here is this: autonomy is not a given; it's provisional.

Tips to use the drawbridge practically:

1. My top tip is to include the drawbridge analogy in your onboarding process to explain how the team member–team leader relationship works. Keep it part of the conversation so staff aren't surprised when you step in if required. That's your job, and poor managers don't fully embrace this responsibility and either overcontrol the drawbridge or don't care at all, making team members proverbially swim the moat.
2. If you're having a tricky time with a team member, use the drawbridge to clearly define the current state of the relationship and use it as a road map to get back to stage four.

3. Use it in coaching for your team members to easily describe relationships with others and how to improve them.

Using the drawbridge can encourage relationships to wake up from an apathetic malaise and transcend it with the power of conscious empathy. Please stop ignoring the fact that we are living, sentient beings. We are all vulnerable individuals who require trusted relationships. We require to be supported with empathy if we're to be successful.

Some companies are just plain ruthless and don't care about the human being. The good news is that there is extraordinary change bubbling up in business. A conscious empathy which is shining into the once cold-hearted approach of many team leaders. It's transforming them into Trust Triangle managers who operate on a level that propels trust skyward, smashing through the low ceiling of short-term productivity gains.

Tools: Sets Clear Expectations

1. Set expectations with team members, not at them. Make sure they're SMART goals.
2. Immediately challenge destructive consent using the Skill Will Model.
3. Use the drawbridge to set clarity around role and expectation

Evidence Based

If you can't measure it, you can't manage it.

—**Peter Drucker**

Once clear expectations have been set you need visual indicators to demonstrate these expectations are being met. Here, you need to satisfy two parties: your team members and your leaders.

Your leaders want to see what you're achieving and struggling with. Are you hitting or missing targets (expectations)? Can you explain why? Make sure you track what you're doing. There's an old saying in American politics: 'Trust but verify.' Leaders want to see the internal data that verifies the performance that you say is happening. Let me be super clear here: seeing evidence of action is not micromanagement. It's best practice. It keeps you and your team accountable. Accountability is the essential ingredient for strong autonomy to flourish. Being open to scrutiny is a basic business expectation. Give your head a shake if you've languished in a silo where accountability is a dirty word. Become more transparent about your progress, problems, and plans. Leaders and team members actually love visual indicators like charts and graphs that clearly demonstrate problems or progress towards the agreed-upon goals.

There are lots of productivity tools like Salesforce, Hubspot, Pipedrive, Jira, Asana (Asana, n.d.) or Trello (Trello, n.d.), depending on your team. Whatever you do please use one. I love Trello. It shows its worth by bucketing tasks in particular projects that are listed in priority. 'To do', 'doing', and 'done' are three basic list headings that not only show that clear expectations are being set but allow everyone to see how they're playing out.

Weekly Report

One great way to understand what's actually happening is to get each team member to compile a weekly report of what they've achieved and what their blockers were. If possible, this should be presented in a team meeting to fellow team members and not just to you, the manager. I strongly suggest you also compile a report. This puts the money where the mouth is and demonstrates to all that you and your team are here to get great work done, together. Here's a great template to use:

Progress: The past, what has been achieved this week.	Problems: What challenges have been encountered.	Plans: The future, what the goals for next week are.

The more open you are about where you are in your expectation, the easier it will be for all parties to become results driven.

I also profoundly disagree with any role that doesn't have clear success metrics set for it. I hear all sorts of excuses. None have ever held much water. How do we know if the team member is at capacity unless we have some idea of what capacity looks like for that role? The team member may be working very hard but the results maybe poor. Without insight, we may accept the poor performance as wonderful! If we don't know what good looks like, how can we measure, appraise, forecast, or hire with certainty that another team member is necessary? How can we truly celebrate success? I am convinced that all team member roles can have some basic KPIs that indicate the level of performance. It's your job as a manager to work out those metrics.

Tools: Evidence Based

1. Insist on visual indicators to show that expectations are being met. Use a productivity management system tool to evidence that expectations are being met. Create charts, graphs, and reports.
2. Implement weekly reports and make sure you do one as well.
3. Clarify what 'working at capacity' looks like for a team member. How do you know that a team member is at capacity if you don't have the metrics to back this up?

Results Driven

According to the consultancy firm Bain, only 12 per cent of companies actually achieve what they set out to accomplish (Bird, Lichtenau, & Michels, 2016).

I have met too many teams who are working hard but delivering little. Have your eyes on the prize every day. I've used the term 'effectiveness over efficiency' earlier in the book and this section demonstrates why effectiveness is just as important as efficiency.

I follow a guy on LinkedIn called Keenan. He's an author and speaker, specialising in sales. We absolutely share the same belief about being results driven.

He goes on to say, 'Stop thinking that I owe you for your effort. It's about what you are delivering with that effort that counts. The currencies are not the same.'

> Your currency to the buyer is results, not hard work.
>
> —Keenan

I passionately believe it's time to stop the grind of 'hard work' and start focusing on being results driven. The reason we're stuck in 'hard work' is, weirdly, apathy. Many managers are not prepared to map out expectations based on accountable evidence. Please spend time on the first two disciplines of the expertise domain to bring absolute clarity to the results you seek. There are a few techniques that can help you stay focused on achieving those results.

Prioritise—Map out the big ones and much on the small ones.

Take time to discover what the most critical tasks are to deliver the greatest result but here's a little trick I learned: head off the little tasks at the same time before they grow too big. So, prioritise the biggies and routinely resolve the smaller ones. I do this by using two techniques. To find the critical tasks, I use the Pareto principle

(Kruse, 2016), and to close out the smaller (often dull) tasks, I use the Pomodoro Technique (Cirillo Consulting GmbH, n.d.).

The Pareto Principle

This is also known as the 80/20 rule and asserts that it will find the vital few things to concentrate on rather than the trivial many. The result being the discovery of the 20 per cent of tasks that deliver the 80 per cent of results.

> Focus on being productive, instead of busy.
>
> —Tim Ferriss

I remember when I worked at BBC Radio. We'd record some audio, broadcast it once, and then throw it away. I found out about the 80/20 rule and started using the audio in many different ways for many different programs. I'd interview someone on the breakfast show. A morning talk show would use a clip from that interview to spark a debate. The whole interview might go out in the evening. We'd chop up the interview and create a package for another show using the callers from the talk show. Therefore, one piece of audio was used several times. Twenty per cent of our effort gave us eighty per cent of our results! The 80/20 rule is awesome. Think about your clothes. You probably wear 20 per cent of your clothes 80 per cent of the time. It's the same in business: find the few critical tasks that yield the best results.

How many times have you had a busy day but achieved little? Re-examine how your day is planned to gain results for as little effort as possible. Think Uber. Imagine one of their taxis driving around a busy city centre all day. Yes, they will be busy and work very hard, *but* if they don't turn on their Uber driver app, they'll never get any fares. It's designed not to allow more than one fare at a time so the taxi won't be swamped with requests and distracted from the task at hand. The taxi driver also uses a GPS to navigate the best route.

These processes are carefully designed to offer optimal delivery of the services that the driver provides.

Being results driven became particularly apparent when I first became a people director. I became very reactive to the myriad daily questions. This, in turn, meant I was spending most of my time on the trivial many rather than the vital few. I then designed a little process. I set up an internal email address for all those little questions and promised that they'd be answered within twenty-four hours. This meant I could manage these issues and resolve, delegate, or defer them far more effectively. This little adjustment saved me a ton of time and allowed me to concentrate on the vital few things. It was just like an Uber driver switching on his app to allow the process to prioritise his workflow.

That's what the Pareto principle aims to do. Its aim is to find those really important things, which are not as many as you'd think.

> Find the critical few from the trivial many.
>
> **—Pareto principle**

Look at what you need to deliver as a manager, and then design ways of working that will specifically deliver those things *and* that can divert the trivial many things. It's a good idea to make a list of those trivial things (as they come up) that are time stealers. In a moment, I'll demonstrate how to work through smaller tasks effectively using the Pomodoro Technique.

Every day, I have a list of three critical things I am going to accomplish to get me closer to the goals I've set. Chop down those big goals to daily goals and drive towards achieving those tasks. This will fan the flame of accomplishment and drive your team to finish what was started, *and* it'll give you, your team, and your leaders insight into how long these things take so you can forecast better next time. This, in turn, will help you set clearer expectations. The better you forecast, the less micromanagement you're going to have to do, as all parties will know what's expected. This is a key to being a great manager. The ability to understand how long a task generally takes. Bad managers don't (or won't) forecast and just leave it up to fate.

I've heard all the excuses under the sun for why it's impossible to measure a task, and most of the time, they hold little merit. All tasks have been done before. How long did they take? How many people did it take to do it? What lessons did they learn? By asking these and other pertinent questions, you'll be able to work out an approximate forecast. Of course, things happen and circumstances change—that's life—but you need to forecast and schedule to map out plans and progress. You'll be amazed at how many managers just don't bother at all. The most legitimate excuse is based on what's called, the cone of uncertainty. It shows how one can estimate a task with increasing accuracy as the details of that task become more apparent over time. My view is this: you can still estimate and then review as more factors come into focus, honing the estimation over time. However, poor managers use the cone of uncertainty as an excuse not to bother planning or estimating at all.

Being results driven means not allowing a culture that is based on wallowing in problems and excuses. It means identifying blockers and working to solve them *with* the team members, not for them. Mindset is everything here, and if the goal is ethereal, too big, or not personal to the team members, then it'll be more difficult to achieve. With trust comes responsibility. So, instil responsibility by allowing them to own the outcome and be recognised for it. Once again shared leadership parades its power.

Pomodoro Technique

It can be difficult to get into a task sometimes. Maybe it's a dreary job that just needs to get done. This technique has really helped me to get started on these tasks and complete them! There's tons of info online; just Google the inventor Francesco Cirillo, and you'll find lots of resources.

This is the technique I use to attack and resolve the smaller tasks.

The basic idea is to constrain your focus to a defined amount of time, usually twenty-five minutes. You turn off or move away from any distractions and super-focus your attention on a particular task. I pledge that I'm going to do at least two 'Pomodoros' a day.

Autonomy

Why should your employees agree to these expertise disciplines that may be perceived as control hell? Well, it's simple: once you set clear expectations that are evidence-based and results driven, autonomy can reign. If the role allows, let them schedule their work time as they please. Flexible working can be implemented. This is the ultimate payoff for a team member. Our aim is the finishing line and not just working hard.

We are basically paid to pay attention to something that we may not normally be as concerned about, if unpaid. So managing your attention is critical to achieving your goals, but be careful not to mix up apathy with focus. They are different beasts. Instead of detaching from your humanity, your attention is simply directed to a task. Moving your focus to a task can be done in an environment of empathy. So please don't use focus as an excuse to operate apathetically. Let people know your preferences. In stand-ups, tell the team you're getting your head down on a task. Talk to your team members about focus, but don't use it as a baseball bat.

Go with the Flow

The workplace has a problem. It's called 'presenteeism'. This can mean being at work when sick or being at work for too long, but it means something else too—millions of workers at their desks watching the clock and not being productive. They may be at work physically, but their minds are someplace else. This costs businesses billions. We need to work with people's energy and not against their flow.

Dan Pink has written an awesome book about this called *When: The Scientific Secrets of Perfect Timing* (Pink, When: The Scientific Secrets of Perfect Timing, 2018). I've always known when I'm at my best, but Pink's spotlight is thoroughly compelling. He demonstrates that most people have a peak, trough, and rebound. He asserts we should do the more challenging analytical tasks during our peak, keep admin for the trough, and then concentrate on the more creative elements of work later in the day. Since I started genuinely putting this into practice, my productivity has been blown out of the water and my general sense of fulfilment has definitely risen. Thanks, Dan!

I can get distracted by doing admin or low-value tasks during my peak, and as a consequence, my analytical tasks are moved later into the day and fall into the trough. That's bad news, as it means I find it really difficult to produce the things I want at the standard and speed I expect. That's super frustrating. The moment this clicked was when I was working with my designer at 10:30 a.m. (my peak). He was sharing his screen, and we were looking at some designs; I was suggesting the logo go 'left a bit … no, a bit more left', and booom! Dan's book came into my mind, and I thought, *what am I doing?* I was literally wasting my peak time on something I could easily do in my trough. So please review when you're in your peak, your trough, and your rebound, and use your finite energy wisely. Draw out your energy chart to understand when you're at your peak, trough, and rebound.

I remember managing a team member who was rubbish before 10 a.m. I am an early bird, and you can find me at my desk at 7:45 a.m., but at that time, this guy was like death warmed up. He'd turn up and it was clear that mornings were not where his energy was. I sat him down and had a frank conversation, making sure there were no underlying issues that needed addressing. There weren't.

He just wasn't great first thing on a morning, and because I was in the office very early, he felt compelled to do the same. I asked him what his perfect day would be. He suggested starting work at 10 a.m., being allowed time to go to the gym at lunch and working later in the evening. I already felt a bit of a failure that he had to use the word 'allow'. I believe in an adult-to-adult relationship at work. We agreed to his suggestions; his productivity increased, and his attitude started to sparkle. We were able to work with his natural energy. This was only possible because we had set clear expectations that were evidence based. If it's possible, people should be able to work the hours they wish. It's not about how hard you work; it's about the results you produce. Not all jobs allow for such flexibility but think about how you can enhance people's power and not drain it.

Some people like buttoned-down plans to work through; others want a more malleable and emergent workflow. If you're building an awesome relationship with your team members, start to notice what lights them up and what drains their energy. Encourage energy by swapping tasks, moving desks, and asking them what they prefer. This is conscious empathy in action. Apathetic leaders and managers just expect their people to trudge on, disregarding their energy levels, but they do so at a cost. Often, the higher the 'rank', the greater the autonomy. Why is that fair? It's just another example of ego and disregard for others, otherwise known as apathy. Once genuine trust is established, please give team members as much autonomy as possible. For example, one of your team members (who you trust) needs to go to the dentist. They shouldn't ask for your permission. They just need to keep you informed. As long as it's in the diary and they've let you know, let them get on with managing their day. This is a classic tell for me in any organisation I work with. So, if I ask 'the dentist question', you'll know what I'm figuring out.

Prioritise—Time is precious. Waste it wisely.

There are only 2,080 working hours a year! Every day, there are tons of data and detritus coming your way. You not only have your own goals to reach, but you are also expected to support your team in reaching theirs. I suggest guarding against being swamped under a daily deluge of stuff that will send you backwards rather than forwards. Believe me, this can happen easily!

The good news is that I have an armoury of awesome techniques to help you in your fight to be productive and not just busy!

The first technique is a great time-management priority tool to classify every request, need, or demand. Decide whether it is something you need to:

- **Do now:** Usually something mission critical or anything that should take less than two minutes. Be careful, though—some 'two-minute tasks' can take two hours.
- **Delegate:** Give to a team member or delegate it to yourself for another time.
- **Defer:** Important but not urgent, like training in three months or some future strategy.
- **Dump:** Useless tasks or info that will bring little or no benefit, like those unrelated marketing emails or silly job offers.

Day by day, you'll get sharper as to which bucket a task will go in. I use Trello and put each of these areas into a list. Other people have a diary and make four columns. The Eisenhower method goes into much more detail about these four areas (Wikipedia, n.d.). Please check it out.

Parkinson's law—work expands to fill the time available (Falconer, n.d.).

This law explains what you already know. How many times have you been in a meeting that is just filling time up until the hour is up? Think of when you've had to buy someone a birthday card. Two scenarios. Firstly, you've nipped out from work to purchase the card; secondly, it's Saturday, and you're mooching around the shops with an hour or two on your hands. The result of both circumstances is that you get a card; however, the difference is how long it takes you to get it. The first scenario, five minutes; the second, two hours.

What Parkinson's law shows is the importance of keeping events short as energy wanes and work expands just to fill the time available.

Parkinson's law

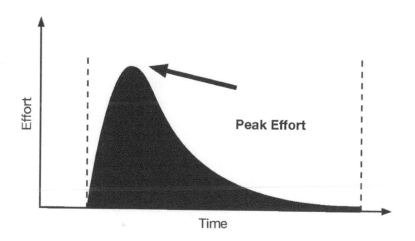

Start making as many meetings as possible thirty minutes instead of an hour. In discussions, stay focused on the topic and don't allow someone else's free time to eat up your precious time!

Managing a Meeting

If you don't keep your meetings on a tight leash, they will run out of control and be of little use. Consider that meetings be conducted under certain conditions for them to be meaningful.

From now on, here's your meeting checklist:

1. Have an agenda and have it sent around before the meeting.
2. Only invite the necessary people.
3. Start on time and finish early.
4. Have someone chair the meeting to keep it on track.
5. Park 'off-topic' discussions.
6. Make sure all attendees are heard.
7. Assign SMART action items as you go and summarise them with the stakeholder's name against them in a follow-up email.
8. No phones—no exception.

Time Stealers

Watch out for these little beggars. They take a few minutes here and there, and you can end up losing hours from your day!

A study of Microsoft workers found that it took fifteen minutes to return to serious mental tasks after an interruption (Lohr, 2007). They reported that interruptions consume an average of 2.1 hours (28 per cent) of every working day.

These interruptions include the likes of:

- Obsessing over checking emails
- Cell phones
- Messenger apps
- Gossip

The ability to focus is paramount for your team members and is a core component of a professional. Make sure the environment is supportive and not obstructive to your ability to focus. If you've got to get some work out of the door, take over a meeting room and make it your war room for the day.

Turn off messenger apps at certain times of the day. If something is business critical, don't worry; someone is sure to tell you.

Block out some time in your calendar that's about getting stuff done and not just being reactive to what's in the air that day. I had a colleague who blocked out 10:30 a.m. until noon and 4 p.m. until 5:30 p.m. every day. He had to move his day around a little occasionally, but he noticed that he gets way more stuff done in that time which could have been consumed by meetings. It's as simple as this: either run your day or your day will run you!

When I think of the Microsoft research and think of, say, a software developer, it reminds me of deep-sea divers. It takes a while to get down to the correct depth, and once they're down there in their world of code, if someone suddenly wrenches them back to the surface, it's like a diver getting the bends. It's no wonder some folks get a little snappy. I hope this analogy helps you understand why it takes time to return to the seabed and why it's sometimes difficult to return to the task at hand due to that distraction. If you want quality work and a good quantity of it, please protect yourself and your team from unnecessary distractions—they're super time stealers.

There are not only extraneous distractions but also internal ones. Here's a great acronym called 'HALT' (Bradford Health Services, n.d.). It stands for:

Hungry: Prone to irrational thinking.

Angry: Reacts rather than responds.

Lonely: Tends to overthink and get lost in your own mind. Can become self-piteous.

Tired: Thinking becomes foggy.

Tools: Results Driven

1. Have (agreed-upon) daily/weekly/monthly targets. Demonstrate in your work the difference between hard work (your internal currency) and results (the external currency).
2. Use the Pareto principle to find the critical few from the trivial many. Use the Pomodoro Technique to munch on the smaller tasks.
3. Minimise distractions by guarding against time stealers that can divert attention from the work at hand. Manage meetings so only necessary people need to be in them and they don't get sidetracked.

MINDFUL MANAGERS

I'm a good man with a good heart

Had a tough time, got a rough start

But I finally learned to let it go

Now I'm right here, and I'm right now

And I'm hoping, knowing somehow

That my shadow days are over

My shadow days are over now

(Mayer, 2012)

Awesome managers are mindful leaders. These people are consciously aware of the impact they have on others because they have a good awareness of themselves. They are deliberate and intentional, with an EQ which allows them to be self and socially congruent. That means when the inner critic (negativity bias) starts with its negative monologue, they have the ability to recognise that these thoughts are theories, much like the prosecution of a criminal case exaggerating some of the more ill-fated decisions the defendant has made in his life. Fortunately, EQ teaches us that there is also a defence. If you've ever been on a jury before, you'll know how compelling one side of the argument is until the other side presents their case. Juries are critical in law because, just left to one person's views, all sorts of biases and moods can have an enormous impact on the fate of a defendant. In fact, as a quick aside, this was shown to be true in some research where judges were found to be more open to the prospect of parole after they had taken a tea break (Bryant, 2011). Hence my caution at a team leader being an all-powerful judge without a jury. Shared leadership brings balance to the power equation, which can otherwise be dominated by one person's outlook or mood.

This chapter starts with some lyrics from the wonderful John Mayer who talks about the shadow days. I have worked with people who cast long shadows and others who bring light into the workplace. Guess which ones were apathetic. You need to protect yourself from apathy—it's contagious! Remember that hurt people will hurt people. Being aware (conscious) of these things is paramount to your success. Mindfulness will help regulate your stress levels, and believe me, it could be the secret to your success as an awesome manager.

Mindfulness is a non-judgmental awareness of the present moment. It's the ability to observe thoughts and not get entangled in them. The evidence is in: mindfulness is incredibly powerful. In fact, a research study published by the University of Oxford a few years back provides evidence of the effectiveness of learning mindfulness (Be Mindful, n.d.).

The study examined the effects of the 'Be Mindful Online' course; and for the 273 people who had completed it, it showed that on average, after one month, they enjoyed:

- A 58 per cent reduction in anxiety levels.
- A 57 per cent reduction in depression.
- A 40 per cent reduction in stress.

Mindfulness takes practice. There are tons of other resources like apps, podcasts, and books to choose from. My recommendation is Mark Williams and Danny Penman's book (Williams & Penman, Mindfulness : A practical guide to finding peace in a frantic world, 2011). Please don't make your mind up after two or three sessions. Rather, give it at least ninety days.

I often explain mindfulness by sharing a visualisation. Imagine you're sitting on a comfortable bench in a large city park on a summer's day. You can hear kids playing in the distance and the birds tweeting in the trees. It's bliss. Then, a man and his small (unleashed) dog walk past you. This cute little dog runs up and barks two or three times at you and then wanders off. You suddenly stand up and manically start following this dog. You're right at his tail as he swerves left and right. The dog starts running faster, turns around, and plays with you, and you are now completely obsessed with keeping up with the dog. The dog gets a bit excited, plays harder, and barks. The owner now comes over and asks, 'What the heck are you doing?'

Freeze the visualisation.

Ask yourself this question: manically chasing a strange dog around the park is obviously crazy—but why?

It's not your dog! And even if it was your dog, you'd allow it to sniff in peace and do its thing without manically chasing it around once it got your attention.

It's not your dog. Yet we do that all the time with thoughts.

A thought will randomly pop into your head, and you'll chase it down, play with it and then complain when it sticks around playing with you!

It was a revelation to me when I discovered how much my mind was controlling my wellbeing. Nowadays, I don't allow many things or people to live in my head rent-free! And I do that by practising mindfulness.

Mindfulness is an ancient practice used in a modern context. Mindfulness is a form of meditation which helps you to centre yourself. Mindfulness is about tuning in, not tuning out. There's a lot of noise in our brains. In the past, wise sages have likened this chattering mind to monkeys.

A client reported to me that worry was still bothering him. Worries about how others saw him, worries about

> Worry often gives a small thing a big shadow.
>
> **—Swedish Proverb**

151

looking stupid, etc. I responded by asking, 'Is it bothering you or are you bothering it?' Now, without sounding like some dodgy Zen wannabe, it's just like the dog in the park. His worries barked a few times and he madly chased them down like some obsessed lunatic. We can be addicted to worry. If it's not tugging away at our peace of mind, like addicts, we need to find it and work ourselves into a state so that we're plunging ourselves back into that familiar place of panic. We must have our 'fix of fear' or we could, God forbid, collapse in a heap of serenity!

I really admire the first nation Americans' ideology on nature and their deep respect for elders. There's a famous American Indian tale of a small boy with his granddad. The boy was recounting a dream he'd had. Two wolves were fighting. One represented peace, the other war. The boy always woke up just before the fight finished. He asked his granddad which wolf would win. The wise old man replied, 'The one you feed.'

And this self-sabotage isn't because we like pain. Unhappiness is not a conscious decision. As I explained at the beginning of this book, the negativity bias is a hard wired protection system but it's pretty redundant in a modern context. You'd be a bit strange to consciously choose to be unhappy. Here's another way of looking at it. I use this visualisation with clients. I call it the 'car analogy'—catchy title, eh? Propulsion can be achieved in two ways. The first and most obvious way is by putting your foot down on the accelerator. The second and often overlooked way is to teach yourself how to take your foot off the brake. I've met so many clients who were holding themselves back and didn't even realise they were doing it. You can be pressing down on the accelerator as well as the brake and wondering why you're just screeching around in circles. The resistance to well-being (your foot on the car brake) starts in your mind, hence the power of mindfulness to manage thoughts that are worrisome and often, frankly, unnecessary.

Anxiety and depression are massive problems. In England, one in six people reports experiencing a common mental health problem (such as anxiety and/or depression) in any given week. These are not numbers; these are real people—your colleagues and maybe even you. Even worse, on average, twelve men take their own lives every day in the UK (Rear, 2019). From financial insecurity to relationship concerns to imposter syndrome and then diagnosed anxiety issues, please do not underestimate the power of the negative mind. Instead of struggling so much, mindfulness asks you to stop, assess, and accept.

> Only when I accept myself, exactly as I am, only then can I change.
>
> **—Carl Rogers**

Carl Rogers is a famous man in psychotherapy circles. He developed a methodology known as person-centred counselling. How on earth will you own any solution if you disagree, struggle, or dismiss the diagnosis? Hence the necessity to consciously and fully accept the situation you're in. And here's another famous dude called Carl with another awesome quote:

> What you resist, persists.
>
> **—Carl Jung**

> When you know yourself, you are empowered. When you accept yourself you are invincible.
>
> **—Tina Lifford**

It is so tempting to wrestle with anxiety, but you do so at your peril. Inadvertently, you have been arming your opponent when you thought you were attacking it. Mindfulness neither attacks nor defends. It simply observes and that's where the power is. It just works.

And Finally ...

Gosh! What a journey. You've come to the end of the book but an end always signals a new beginning, right? It's now time for you to consistently apply *The Trust Triangle* into your business life.

It is always a privilege to share a manager's journey using *The Trust Triangle* and see change manifest and emotional intelligence grow. Thank you from the bottom of my heart for having the courage to make that change.

For some, this program is out of reach. They will be nowhere near ready to embark on *The Trust Triangle*. Their fake facades will be firmly fastened onto their pretend personalities and their multi-pronged defences will be on full alert. Remember where all this defensiveness comes from (the negativity bias and the primal wound). Be patient if you're working with these people and please tread gently. If that person is you, it's time to let those defences down and thrive in the workplace because now you have the tools.

I sincerely wish you every success when implementing this program into your work life. Change is never easy but please keep an open mind and go for it!

> Change is inevitable. Growth is optional.
>
> **—John C. Maxwell**

Checklist for Change

We're told that forty-two is the magic number. Please find (below) forty-two practical tips, tools, and techniques. These were all mentioned in the book. Make sure you're applying these in your work practice. I see it as a successful intervention if a team leader consistently practises at least ten of these actions.

1. Learn *The Trust Triangle* methodology. If you don't learn it, you won't be able to live it.
2. It takes time to create a new habit (sixty-six days). Commit to *The Trust Triangle* program by:
   - Routine: Set aside ten minutes every day to learn this program.
   - Reward: Implement this program asap and chronicle your successes. It will motivate you to practice this more.
   - Reminder: Tell your manager what you're doing so you have an accountability partner.

3. Take a personality test to increase self-awareness. Check out MBTI (The Myers-Briggs Company, n.d.) or Gallup StrengthsFinder (Gallup, n.d.).
4. Remember it's not the crime, it's the cover up. Get real about facing conflict and not avoiding it. Remember conflict is inevitable but combat is optional.
5. Strengthen your emotional intelligence muscles. Use the Johari window, and remember, when emotions are high, cognitive functioning is low. When you get angry, you get stupid. There are tons of resources. Check out the book *Emotional Intelligence 2.0,* which also includes an EQ assessment.
6. Take a blank piece of A4. Create two columns. Think of someone at work (or who you've worked with in the past) that you really trust. Write down their qualities. In the other

column, think about someone at work you really don't trust. Write down the characteristics that made you distrust them. Are you truly practising what you admire? If not, why not?

7. Get a journal and write down your challenges and successes while working this program. Please handwrite this. It's known to be cathartic.

8. Remember to connect first. That will build trust to collaborate effectively. Don't collaborate as a way to deeply connect. It doesn't work. Embrace the power of small talk but use it to go deeper. Don't stay in the shallows of small talk.

9. Start fortnightly 121s with your team members. Thirty to sixty minutes, dependent on role and industry. Walk and talk. Go to a cafe. Agree on a book you're both going to read and chat about it every time you meet. Ask about their family. Connect with their humanity. Only cancel if absolutely necessary. Rebook instantly. They will judge their value to you on how much time you spend with them, one on one.

10. Learn to listen. Use the ARC technique. Remember: when others feel heard by you, they're more likely to listen to you.

11. Be mindful of and learn to embrace your 'thug'—your negative bias. Professor Steve Peters called the thug a chimp in his awesome book *The Chimp Paradox* (Peters, 2012). Please read it.

12. Download a mindfulness app and start practising to become mindful of your apathy versus empathy responses. Mindfulness helps build your attention muscles and turn your attention where you wish rather than to any whim.

13. Implement shared leadership tools to encourage accountability. Remember those closest to the problem are most motivated to fix it.

14. Stop playing 'boss'. Be in the team not above it.

15. Create an environment of psychological safety by working *The Trust Triangle* into the workplace and doing these things:
    - Approach conflict as a collaborator – emotional intelligence, not as an adversary – negativity bias.
    - Promote effectiveness as much as efficiency.

16. Celebrate success by starting a monthly/quarterly 'wheel of wow'. Ask for nominations from team members for others who've gone the extra mile or done great work. Spin the wheel and allocate prizes. Have some fun prizes. You can also read out nominations then put them in a hat and pull out one as the winner. You're celebrating success and having some fun at the same time.

17. Use the drawbridge for onboarding and coaching to create a better understanding for managing professional relationships and the flow of trust.

18. Set expectations with team members, not at them. Make sure they're SMART goals.

19. Set expectations and play them back to team members to clarify their understandings.

20. Make sure you're hiring team members with intrinsic motivation. Do a pulse check in your 121s to see if intrinsic motivation is high.

21. Always have visual indicators of progress. Use a productivity tool to evidence expectations being met. Check out Trello.

22. Clarify what 'working at capacity' looks like for a team member. How do you know that a team member is at capacity if you don't have the metrics to back this up?

23. Implement weekly reports, and make sure you do one as well.
    - Progress
    - Problems
    - Plans

24. Focus on results. Have daily/weekly/monthly targets to hit and gamify the experience.
25. Break the golden rule and treat others the way *they'd* like to be treated. Ask for their communication preferences.
26. Be mindful of the Drama Triangle. Don't rescue, coach.
27. Boost a growth mindset by encouraging consistent learning opportunities.
28. Map out where your team members are in the Skill Will model and confront the cynics.
29. Remember Herzberg. Learn the difference between hygiene and motivational factors. Deliver on both.
30. Create energy charts for each team member. Where's their peak, trough, and rebound?
31. Manage meetings using all the tips in the book.
32. Be mindful of Parkinson's law: time expands to fill the time available.
33. Use the Pareto principle to find the critical few from the trivial many. Use the Pomodoro Technique to munch on the smaller tasks.
34. Find the time stealers and minimise them.
35. Consistently apply the 4X Feedback Model.
36. Pushing versus pulling. Be a puller rather than a pusher.
37. Make presentations into conversations by interacting. Be interested and not just interesting.
38. Apply all the preparation and performance tips to your presentations, like:
    - AIDA technique
    - Inform and motivate
    - Research, review, rehearse

39. Use these techniques to manage up effectively:
    - Ask for their communication preferences.
    - Bring solutions to problems.
    - They don't like surprises.

40. Put together a personal development plan (PDP) with each team member.
41. Use the GROW model to navigate coaching interventions.
42. Stay conscious of being in the present moment rather than the fear of times past or to come. Read Eckhart Tolle's book *The Power of Now.*

There are tons more resources available on the website at www.thetrusttriangle.com

REFERENCES

AMA. (2019, January 24). *In Business Nice Guys Finish First.* Retrieved from The American Management Association | AMA: https://www.amanet.org/articles/new-study-shows-nice-guys-finish-first/

Asana. (n.d.). *Asana.* Retrieved from Asana: https://asana.com/

Barsade, S. (2014, October 15). *Faster Than a Speeding Text: "Emotional Contagion" at Work.* Retrieved from Psychology Today: https://www.psychologytoday.com/gb/blog/the-science-work/201410/faster-speeding-text-emotional-contagion-work

Be Mindful. (n.d.). *The Evidence.* Retrieved from Be Mindful: https://www.bemindfulonline.com/evidence

Beck, R. J., & Harter, J. (2014, March 25). *Why Great Managers Are So Rare.* Retrieved from Gallup: https://www.gallup.com/workplace/231593/why-great-managers-rare.aspx

Bird, A., Lichtenau, T., & Michels, D. (2016, February 9). *The What, Who and How of Delivering Results.* Retrieved from Bain & Company: https://www.bain.com/insights/what-who-and-how-of-delivering-results/

Bradford Health Services. (n.d.). *HALT: The Dangers of Hunger, Anger, Loneliness, and Tiredness.* Retrieved from Bradford Health Services: https://bradfordhealth.com/halt-hunger-anger-loneliness-tiredness/

Bregman, P. (2018). *Leading With Emotional Courage: How to Have Hard Conversations, Create Accountability, And Inspire Action on Your Most Important Work*. New York: John Wiley & Sons Inc.

Bryant, B. (2011, April 11). *Judges are more lenient after taking a break, study finds*. Retrieved from The Guardian: https://www.theguardian.com/law/2011/apr/11/judges-lenient-break

Businessolver. (n.d.). *State of Workplace Empathy*. Retrieved from Businessolver: https://www.businessolver.com/resources/state-of-workplace-empathy

CFI. (n.d.). *SMART Goal - Definition, Guide, and Importance of Goal Setting*. Retrieved from Corporate Finance Institute | CFI: https://corporatefinanceinstitute.com/resources/knowledge/other/smart-goal/

Cirillo Consulting GmbH. (n.d.). *The Pomodoro Technique*. Retrieved from Cirillo Consulting GmbH: https://francescocirillo.com/pages/pomodoro-technique

Coleman, A. (2017, October 26). *What are the benefits of collaboration in the workplace?* Retrieved from Telegraph: https://www.telegraph.co.uk/business/open-economy/benefits-of-collaboration/

Craig, W. (2017, January 10). *Further Evidence That Trust Is the No. 1 Ingredient For a Strong Company Culture*. Retrieved from Forbes: https://www.forbes.com/sites/williamcraig/2017/01/10/further-evidence-that-trust-is-the-no-1-ingredient-for-a-strong-company-culture/

Duzyj, M. (Director). (2019). *Losers* [Motion Picture].

Engage for Success. (2013, February 19). *The Evidence*. Retrieved from Engage for Success: https://engageforsuccess.org/the-evidence

Engage for Success. (2014, May 15). *Boost NHS Employee Engagement to Save Lives, Says IPA*. Retrieved from Engage for Success: https://engageforsuccess.org/boost-nhs-employee-engagement-to-save-lives-says-ipa

Falconer, J. (n.d.). *How to Use Parkinson's Law to Your Advantage.* Retrieved from Lifehack: https://www.lifehack.org/articles/featured/how-to-use-parkinsons-law-to-your-advantage.html

Firman, J., & Gila, A. (1997). *The Primal Wound: A Transpersonal View of Trauma, Addiction, and Growth.* Albany: State University of New York Press.

Fisher, R., & Ury, W. (2012). *Getting to Yes : Negotiating an agreement without giving in.* London: Cornerstone.

Frei, F. (2018, April). *Frances Frei: How to build (and rebuild) trust | TED Talk.* Retrieved from TED: https://www.ted.com/talks/frances_frei_how_to_build_and_rebuild_trust

Gallup. (n.d.). *CliftonStrengths Online Talent Assessment.* Retrieved from Gallup: https://www.gallup.com/cliftonstrengths/en/252137/home.aspx

Glouberman, S., & Zimmerman, B. (2002, July). *The Canadian health care system was an improtant ingredient of Canadian federalism for twenty years.* Retrieved from Government of Canada Publications: http://publications.gc.ca/collections/Collection/CP32-79-8-2002E.pdf

Goleman, D. (2007). *Emotional Intelligence.* New York: Random House USA Inc.

Goleman, D. (2017, March). *Daniel Goleman: Why aren't we more compassionate? | TED Talk.* Retrieved from TED: https://www.ted.com/talks/daniel_goleman_why_aren_t_we_more_compassionate

Hari, J. (2018). *Lost Connections : Why You're Depressed and How to Find Hope.* London: Bloomsbury Publishing PLC.

IDEO U. (n.d.). *Power of Purpose Online Course.* Retrieved from IDEO U: https://www.ideou.com/products/power-of-purpose

Jaworski, M. (2019, May 23). *The Negativity Bias: Why the Bad Stuff Sticks and How to Overcome It.* Retrieved from Psycom: https://www.psycom.net/negativity-bias

Karpman, S. (2014). *A Game Free Life: The New Transactional Analysis of Intimacy, Openness, and Happiness.* San Francisco: Drama Triangle Publications.

KNILT. (n.d.). *Crisis as an Opportunity.* Retrieved from KNILT: https://knilt.arcc.albany.edu/Crisis_as_an_Opportunity

Kruse, K. (2016, March 7). *The 80/20 Rule And How It Can Change Your Life.* Retrieved from Forbes: https://www.forbes.com/sites/kevinkruse/2016/03/07/80-20-rule/

Laurence, P. J., & Hull, R. (1994). *The Peter Principle: Why Things Always Go Wrong.* London: Profile Books Ltd.

Lencioni, P. M. (2002). *The Five Dysfunctions of a Team : A Leadership Fable.* New York: John Wiley & Sons Inc.

Lohr, S. (2007, March 25). *Slow Down, Brave Multitasker, and Don't Read This in Traffic.* Retrieved from The New York Times: https://www.nytimes.com/2007/03/25/business/25multi.html

MacLeod, D., & Clarke, N. (2009, July). *Engaging for success: enhancing performance through employee engagement.* Retrieved from Engage for Success: https://engageforsuccess.org/wp-content/uploads/2015/08/file52215.pdf

Mayer, J. (2012). Shadow Days [Recorded by J. Mayer]. USA.

McLeod, S. (2018). *Maslow's Hierarchy of Needs.* Retrieved from Simply Psychology: https://www.simplypsychology.org/maslow.html

Mental Health Foundation. (n.d.). *Mental health statistics: stress.* Retrieved from Mental Health Foundation: https://www.mentalhealth.org.uk/statistics/mental-health-statistics-stress

MindTools. (n.d.). *5 Whys.* Retrieved from MindTools: https://www.mindtools.com/pages/article/newTMC_5W.htm

MindTools. (n.d.). *Forming, Storming, Norming, and Performing.* Retrieved from MindTools: https://www.mindtools.com/pages/article/newLDR_86.htm

MindTools. (n.d.). *The GROW Model of Coaching and Mentoring.* Retrieved from MindTools: https://www.mindtools.com/ pages/article/newLDR_89.htm

Norwich University. (n.d.). *Emotional Intelligence (EQ) and Leadership.* Retrieved from Norwich University Online: https://online.norwich.edu/academic-programs/masters/ leadership/resources/infographics/emotional-intelligence- eq-and-leadership

Oesch, T. (2018, November 13). *Managing End-of-Year Stress in the Workplace.* Retrieved from Training Industry: https://trainingindustry.com/articles/compliance/ managing-end-of-year-stress-in-the-workplace/

Pagano, A., & Kakoyiannis, A. (2017, November 21). *What Steve Jobs was like to work with.* Retrieved from Business Insider: https://www.businessinsider.com/steve-jobs-andy- cunningham-fired-terrible-work-loved-anyway-2017-11

Pangarkar, N. (2012, March 5). *A failure of focus: Lessons from Kodak.* Retrieved from Think Business: https://thinkbusiness.nus. edu.sg/article/kodak/

Peters, S. (2012). *The Chimp Paradox: How Our Impulses and Emotions Can Determine Success and Happiness and How We Can Control Them.* London: Ebury Press.

Pink, D. H. (2011). *Drive : The Surprising Truth About What Motivates Us.* Edinburgh: Canongate Books Ltd.

Pink, D. H. (2018). *When: The Scientific Secrets of Perfect Timing.* Melbourne: Text Publishing.

Porath, C., & Pearson, C. (2013, February). *The Price of Incivility.* Retrieved from Harvard Business Review: https://hbr. org/2013/01/the-price-of-incivility

PwC. (n.d.). *Putting Purpose to Work.* Retrieved from PwC: https:// www.pwc.com/us/en/purpose-workplace-study.html

Rear, J. (2019, November 19). *International Men's Day 2019: the shocking statistics you need to know.* Retrieved from The Telegraph: https://www.telegraph.co.uk/health-fitness/

mind/international-mens-day-2018-shocking-statistics-need-know/

Scott, K. (2018). *Radical Candor*. London: Pan Books.

Seppälä, E. (2012, August 26). *Connect to Thrive*. Retrieved from Psychology Today UK: https://www.psychologytoday.com/gb/blog/feeling-it/201208/connect-thrive

Sinek, S. (2011). *Start with Why: How Great Leaders Inspire Everyone to Take Action*. New York: Penguin Putnam Inc.

Sinek, S. (2018). *Leaders Eat Last: Why Some Teams Pull Together and Others Don't*. London: Penguin Books Ltd.

TED. (2009, September). *Simon Sinek: How Great Leaders Inspire Action | TED Talk*. Retrieved from TED: https://www.ted.com/talks/simon_sinek_how_great_leaders_inspire_action

The HALO Trust. (n.d.). *A Precious Harvest Among the Landmines*. Retrieved from The HALO Trust: https://www.halotrust.org/latest/halo-updates/stories/a-precious-harvest-among-the-landmines/

The Karpman Drama Triangle. (n.d.). *The Official Site of the Karpman Drama Triangle Home Page*. Retrieved from The Official Site of the Karpman Drama Triangle: https://karpmandramatriangle.com/

The Myers-Briggs Company. (n.d.). *The Myers-Briggs Company Homepage*. Retrieved from The Myers-Briggs Company: https://eu.themyersbriggs.com/

The Peak Performance Center. (n.d.). *The Skill Will Matrix*. Retrieved from The Peak Performance Center: http://thepeakperformancecenter.com/business/coaching/skill-will-matrix/

The RSA. (2013, December 10). *Brené Brown on Empathy | The RSA*. Retrieved from YouTube: https://www.youtube.com/watch?v=1Evwgu369Jw

Torres, D. (2007, September 11). *Some bad boss statistics*. Retrieved from Management-Issues: https://www.management-issues.com/news/4485/some-bad-boss-statistics/

Trello. (n.d.). *Trello.* Retrieved from Trello: https://trello.com/

Trotta, J. (2018, December 10). *Emotional Intelligence — What Do the Numbers Mean?* Retrieved from LinkedIn: https://www.linkedin.com/pulse/emotional-intelligence-what-do-numbers-mean-joanne-trotta/

UCL. (2009, August 4). *How long does it take to form a habit?* Retrieved from UCL: https://www.ucl.ac.uk/news/2009/aug/how-long-does-it-take-form-habit

Visceral Business. (2013, June 16). *Seth Godin at SAP: The Connection Economy - Why it Matters.* Retrieved from Vimeo: https://vimeo.com/68470240

Wagner, R. (2018, April 10). *New Evidence the Peter Principle Is Real - And What to Do About It.* Retrieved from Forbes: https://www.forbes.com/sites/roddwagner/2018/04/10/new-evidence-the-peter-principle-is-real-and-what-to-do-about-it/

Wax, R. (2019). *How to Be Human: The Manual.* London: Penguin Books Ltd.

WHO. (2018, March 22). *Depression.* Retrieved from WHO | World Health Organization: https://www.who.int/news-room/fact-sheets/detail/depression

Wikipedia. (n.d.). *AIDA (marketing).* Retrieved from Wikipedia: https://en.wikipedia.org/wiki/AIDA_(marketing)

Wikipedia. (n.d.). *Johari window.* Retrieved from Wikipedia: https://en.wikipedia.org/wiki/Johari_window

Wikipedia. (n.d.). *Time management.* Retrieved from Wikipedia: https://en.wikipedia.org/wiki/Time_management#The_Eisenhower_Method

Wikipedia. (n.d.). *Two-factor theory.* Retrieved from Wikipedia: https://en.wikipedia.org/wiki/Two-factor_theory

Williams, J. G., & Penman, D. (2011). *Mindfulness : A practical guide to finding peace in a frantic world.* London: Little, Brown Book Group.

Williams, J. G., Teasdale, J., Segal, Z. V., & Kabat-Zinn, J. (2007). *The Mindful Way through Depression: Freeing Yourself from Chronic Unhappiness.* New York: Guilford Publications.

Zak, P. J. (2018). *Trust Factor: The Science of Creating High-Performance Companies.* Nashville: Harpercollins Focus.

Zenger, J. (2012, December 17). *We Wait Too Long to Train Our Leaders.* Retrieved from Harvard Business Review: https://hbr.org/2012/12/why-do-we-wait-so-long-to-trai

AUTHOR: MATTHEW DAVIES

Matthew consults as a part-time people director, leadership coach, and learning and development specialist. He sees, first-hand, the struggles unskilled managers have when dealing with their team members. He has concluded that trust is the ultimate roadblock. Matthew hunted high and low for an appropriate solution but couldn't find a suitable training program to practically and powerfully resolve the trust issue. This compelled him to develop *The Trust Triangle* and ultimately write this book. He spends all his time in companies working this methodology and the results have been extraordinary. Matthew's approach opens the door to a workplace where collaboration eclipses control, all built on the power of trust.

Before *The Trust Triangle*, he founded Power the Change, a people development practice based in London. Matthew has worked with thousands of professionals, mainly in Europe and the USA. He is an accredited coach who has worked for some of the most exciting businesses on the planet: companies from the likes of Just Eat, Vodafone, Stripe, and moo.com.

A member of coaching at the Association of Coaching, CIPD, and a Fellow of the Learning and Performance Institute, his unmistakable energy creates a powerful environment for change.

Although Matthew takes his role seriously, he likes to experience life with a light heart, so expect a smile if you encounter him.

Matthew Davies in action: